REMEMBERING

Steubenville

REMEMBERING

Steubenville

FROM FRONTIER FORT TO STEEL VALLEY

DR. JOHN R. HOLMES

The History PRESS

Published by The History Press
Charleston, SC 29403
www.historypress.net

First published 2009

Manufactured in the United States

ISBN 978.1.59629.645.9

Library of Congress Cataloging-in-Publication Data

Holmes, John R. (John Robert), 1955-
Remembering Steubenville : from frontier fort to steel valley / John R. Holmes.
p. cm.
Includes bibliographical references.
ISBN 978-1-59629-645-9
1. Steubenville (Ohio)--History. 2. Steubenville (Ohio)--Social life and customs. I. Title.
F499.S8H65 2009
977.1'69--dc22
2009019599

Contents

Acknowledgements

Some of the stories in this book may already sound familiar. Well, isn't that the nature of stories that old guys tell? You hear the same ones over and over again. Members of the Steubenville Women's Club will recognize much of the Female Seminary material in this book from a play I did for them in 1998 (with my talented wife, Von, playing Hetty Beatty) and then again as a lecture in 2005. Material on the nineteenth-century industrialists of Steubenville was performed for the Jefferson County Historical Society in 1992 (also with Von's help). This book, then, owes a great deal to those groups for being preview audiences.

It also owes much, probably even more than I am aware, to the late Professor Jack Boyde of Franciscan University of Steubenville. He was a constant resource and a source of encouragement as I was first learning about this quirky and fascinating river town. Also to Dick and Elizabeth King, the driving force behind the building of Fort Steuben, making history live in Steubenville.

The sections on Fred and Dorothy Sloop are heavily indebted to conversations with clarinet virtuoso Harry Greenburg, who played with both Sloops. I hope you publish your memoirs, Harry.

But most of all, especially in the production stage of this book, the greatest debt is to the Public Library of Steubenville and Jefferson County, especially Director Alan Hall and Archivist Sandy Day. A visit to the Ohio Room at the Schiappa Branch of the PLSJC will reveal just how little this book owes to its writer and how much to the tireless labor of Alan and Sandy and their colleagues. The raw material for hundreds of books like this are in the Ohio Room. Even I can't write that much.

Introduction

I have no childhood memories of Steubenville, Ohio. Is that odd? Hardly. Because I was thirty-four years old before I even visited the city. Yet within three years of my arrival I was immersed in its history. Portraying Baron von Steuben for the first Fort Steuben Festival in 1991, I found myself in the delightful (but maybe presumptuous) position of telling Steubenville natives about their own history.

This book represents one more whack at that same audacity: an amateur historian who "ain't from around here" presuming to tell what it was like here way back when. Begging the reader's indulgence, I plead in my defense only the fact that most of the best stories in this book took place before any of the readers were born. So at least I am shielded from the charge of telling natives things that they ought to know better than I. Furthermore, most of the best stories are not the kind of legacies likely to be passed on from earlier generations. Great-grandmother's bonnet might survive in mothballs in your closet as a family treasure, but the details of where she bought it and whose attention she hoped it would attract are no doubt lost to time. Especially since she probably didn't want great-grandfather to know.

To show you what I mean, I'll tell a story—the first of many in this book. When I first spoke to the Steubenville Historical Society early in 1993, the big topic of conversation at the meeting was the impending demolition of the Hub. This aptly named department store had been the epicenter of Steubenville mercantile activity since—well, since before anybody in the room could remember. Now, despite the actions of several historical society members then present, the building that housed the store—abandoned since 1980—was about to be torn down. The store had closed five years before I came to Steubenville, so I had nothing to add to the conversation,

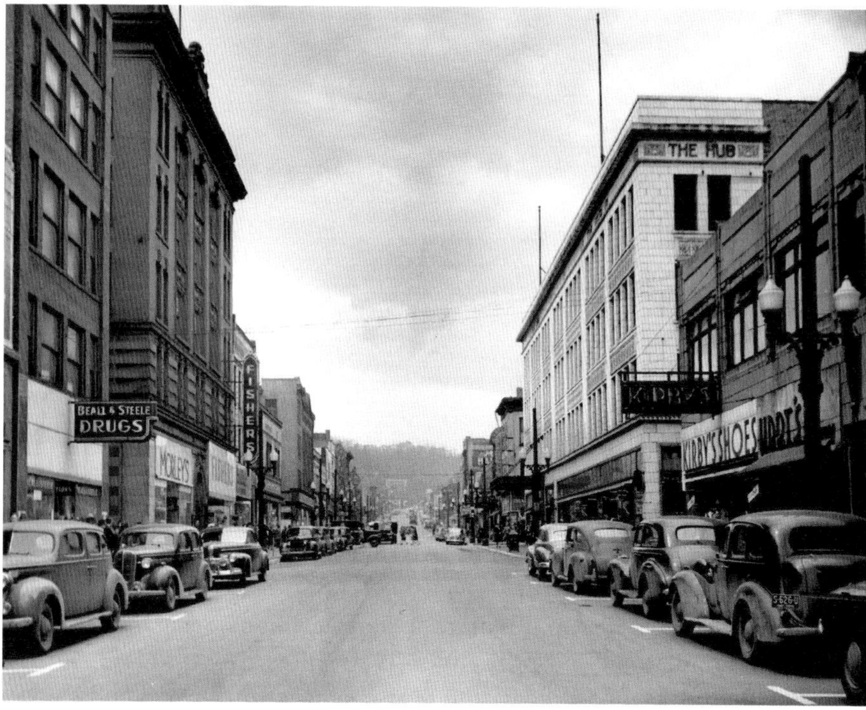

Market Street looking west toward Fifth Street, 1947, with the Hub at right. *Ohio Collection, Schiappa Library.*

but my kindly hosts insisted on knowing my opinion of this turn of events. "Well," I ventured, "I'm sure that the people of Steubenville who grew up with Munker's and Sulzbacher's must have felt the same sense of loss when they closed."

Blank stares. Wrinkled foreheads. "Munker's? Sulzbacher's? Who are they?" Then a few of the postcard aficionados remembered seeing an old tinted photocard of a Market Street scene showing the Hub on the left and Sulzbacher's on the right. But no one had heard of Munker's. Now, keep in mind, I was sharing a banquet table with lifelong residents of Steubenville, some of whom were third-generation residents (or more), whose grandparents must have shopped at both Sulzbacher's and Munker's only a century before. Yet scarcely any of them recognized the names of two high-volume Steubenville stores that once boasted buyer's offices in London and Paris. I had chosen those names because I had naively assumed that they would be part of my hosts' family memories. They clearly were not.

On reflection, however, with the hindsight of years, the blank expressions made sense. It is precisely the simple, everyday activity like shopping at Munker's that will *not* become part of family memory or even a city's consciousness. But the one day that President-elect Lincoln came to Steubenville (Valentine's Day 1861), the big parade that welcomed Dean Martin (and Jerry Lewis) to Dean Martin Day (October 6, 1950) or the day "Buffalo Bill" Cody brought his "Buffalo Bill's Wild West" show to the Hill-Top Driving Park—those are things to tell your grandchildren.

That, in fact, is what I'm trying to offer in this book: the stories I would have told my grandchildren if I had grown up in Steubenville back in the day—when steamboats built right here plied the Ohio, run by Steubenville captains; when city council had its own one-thousand-seat opera house; and when Steubenville's armchair sportsmen tipped back a bottle of Steuben Brew™ and debated (seriously) whether the new roller-skating craze would spell the end to baseball in the Ohio Valley (this was the fall of 1868). The late, great Ohio Valley historian and archaeologist, Professor Jack Boyde, used to taunt me by saying that I was only an English teacher *pretending* to be a historian. He was right. I am a storyteller, and these are my Steubenville stories, set in a historical frame. As such, they have no claim to comprehensiveness.

A century ago, Joseph B. Doyle published his history of Steubenville and Jefferson County at nearly 1,200 pages and about 800,000 words. With 128 pages and about 35,000 words—4 percent of Doyle's space, with twice as much history to cover—this book has to be more selective. There will be very important Steubenville characters and events left out. In fact, some of the better-known stories were intentionally left out precisely because they are so well known and told elsewhere. But that still leaves a lot of tidbits that haven't been related in years. I'm sure you'll find one you'll like. Pull up a chair. Pour some tea. Read a bit.

Okay, are you ready? We'll start with the "Four Fs" of Steubenville: the Frontier, the Fort, the Founding and the First Federal Land Office. Does "First Federal" make it Five Fs? I don't know. Either way, here we go.

PART I
The Pioneer Settlement

The Frontier

The earliest stories of Steubenville boil down to this question (with apologies to Gertrude Stein): what was here before there was a "here" here? Before there was a Steubenville (or even a Fort Steuben, but we'll get to that later), what was this bluff overlooking the Ohio River like? Who were those first European interlopers making audacious claims on untouched forests?

In this particular spot that we now call Steubenville, evidence suggests that even some of the Native Americans encountered by the English and French traders had come from somewhere else. Of the earliest Native American families we have no stories to hand down—they died or were pushed out by the migration of eastern tribes long before the coming of the "long knives" (as the Native American tribes in the upper Ohio Valley called the Europeans, due to the swords they wore). The "Beaver Wars" of 1650–1700 sent various nations of the Iroquois Confederacy into this area, killing or routing any inhabitants. Then the Leni-Lenape (known to the French and English as the Delaware) seem to have settled in this region by 1740, though the southern reach of their settlements may not have come as far as Steubenville.

The Iroquois (mostly Seneca) who stayed here became known as the Mingo, and by the middle of the eighteenth century there were tenuous Mingo settlements upriver and downriver from the Steubenville bluff but apparently none where the town itself would be. Upstream (at Yellow Creek) was the hunting camp of Chief Logan, where his family was savagely murdered in 1774; downstream was "Mingo Town," where the captive Mary Jemison was brought from Philadelphia in 1755. George Washington visited descendants of the Iroquois at Mingo in 1770 and reported some twenty cabins there. But a generation earlier (August 12, 1749), when Captain Louis Celeron de Bienville sailed by, he saw no trace of either settlement—though who knows how hard he tried.

The first attempts to settle in Steubenville proper were acts of trespass not only by Native American standards, but also by English colonial law. These settlers were, to use the colloquialism, "squatters." We don't expect accounts of our ancestors' criminal acts to survive in family stories. Oddly enough, though, that's exactly what we get. When Joseph Doyle compiled his massive *Twentieth Century History of Steubenville and Jefferson County* in 1910, he recorded a descendant's account of his great-grandfather's "tomahawk claim" of land that would not become Steubenville until twenty-two years later.

In 1765, Jacob Walker, after clearing land for a farm on the Virginia side, crossed the river to stake out a claim at what was called "Marsh's Spring" in nineteenth-century Steubenville (and modern-day North Seventh Street, by Doyle's estimate). The Walker family legend, as Doyle recorded it, had Jacob Walker building a cabin here in the summer of 1765, returning to his native Baltimore to marry Margaret Guthrie and bringing her to the cabin in August 1766. Great-grandpa Walker claimed to have watched the building of Fort Steuben in 1787 and to have been present at the death of

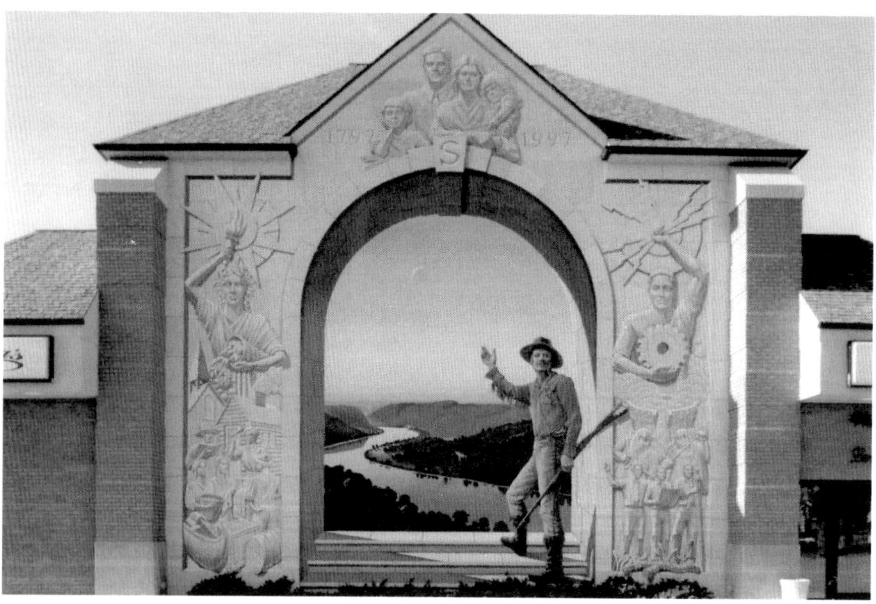

A Bicentennial image from Steubenville's "City of Murals" project, 1997, depicting a Steubenville pioneer of 1797. *Steubenville Murals, Inc.*.

Captain Buskirk in the summer of 1793. Buskirk had raised a thirty-man posse, including Walker, to avenge the death of his wife and son in an Indian raid the previous year. Captain Buskirk himself died in that raid, but Walker lived to tell the tale to his children and grandchildren.

The next squatters we hear of in Steubenville come a generation after Walker—at a time when the new federal government of the infant United States was cracking down on squatters. The American treasury was counting on sale of the Ohio lands to pay its enormous war debts from the Revolution. The army's first task, then, was to remove all inhabitants by force to prepare for the land surveyors. Of the thirty-four family names recorded as removed between Little Beaver (present-day East Liverpool) and Wheeling, only three were in what is now Steubenville: Boley, Waddle and Castleman. All three moved on down the river to stay ahead of the feds, though John Boley shows up on the federal payroll with the Lewis and Clark voyage of discovery in 1804. Of the Castlemans a few additional words survive.

On April 3, 1785, Ensign John Armstrong of the First American Regiment encountered John Castleman, his brother Jacob and Jacob's son, Andrew, on their homestead on a flat terrace "two mile above Mingo Town." Other squatters (unnamed) simply fled, but these three filed a grievance with the U.S. Congress. Jacob and Andrew settled on the Virginia side, but John returned to the charred outline of his cabin and rebuilt, only to have his second cabin burned by Captain John Francis Hamtramck exactly one year later, on April 3, 1786. John gave up and moved to Tennessee, but one last story kept the Castleman name alive in Steubenville into the next century.

Jacob Castleman may not have tried to build or farm on the Ohio side ever again, but his daughters, Margaret and Mary, were lured there by the prospect of Ohio maple sugar. Boiling maple sap on the Ohio side, under the protection of a man named Martin, they were surprised by a party of Indians, who killed Martin and captured Mary. Margaret eluded the attack, but instead of running home to safety, she followed the captors and was herself taken. The girls were brought to Sandusky, where Margaret was sold to a French trader. Jacob later found his daughter in Detroit and brought her back to her Ohio Valley home. Mary, married to an Indian who constantly threatened her with a knife, escaped when he finally threw it at her, and she made her way back here. Both Castleman girls married and settled in Jefferson County—as soon as there was a Jefferson County—which is why the story remained a local legend.

THE FORT

The same man who burned out the Castlemans (twice) would turn out to be, indirectly, the man who gave Steubenville its name. John Francis Hamtramck was born in Quebec of Belgian parents and grew up with the French *voyageurs* who traded with the Indians throughout North America. When the American colonies declared independence, Hamtramck was a nineteen-year-old with a Francophone's natural antipathy toward English authority; he was recruited by Lewis DuBois for the Fifth New York Regiment with the rank of captain. Ten years later he found himself here in the Ohio Valley, charged with protecting the government surveyors. To do so, on October 11, 1786, he built a blockhouse in the clearing made by Boley, Waddle and Castleman. When that single blockhouse proved inadequate to protect the 150 men under his command, more than one-fifth of the entire U.S. Army at that time, Hamtramck received permission to build a full-fledged fort, with four blockhouses and a palisade of pickets.

With one blockhouse already standing, Hamtramck needed his three companies to build three more blockhouses. Three companies. Three blockhouses. The math was irresistible. Hamtramck suggested a contest.

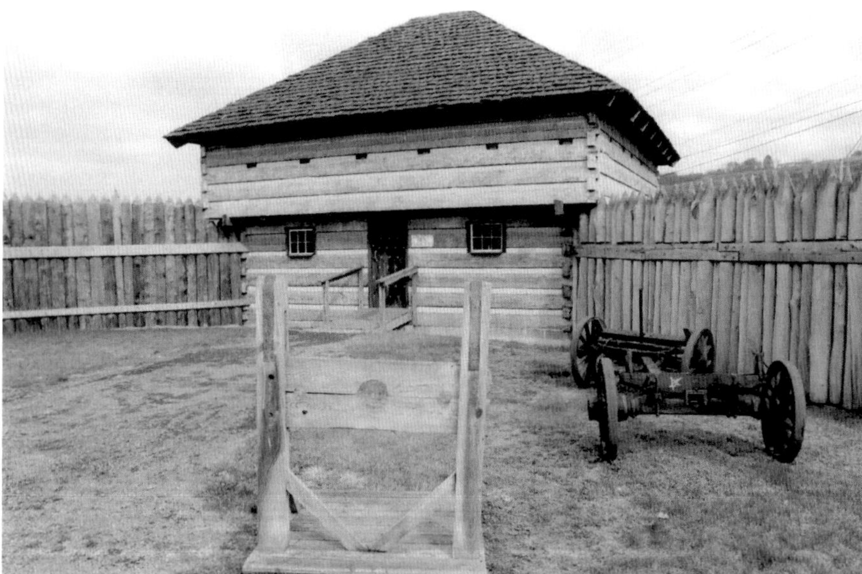

Blockhouse and pickets at Fort Steuben, the modern reconstruction of the 1787 fort. *Ohio Collection, Schiappa Library.*

Whichever company finished a blockhouse first would win a prize. But what prize? The usual military currency, furlough, was out of the question as there was no place to go, and the government was broke, so no monetary prize. The soldiers would be lucky to get their pay. Then Hamtramck hit on the universal frontier motivator: whiskey.

Six gallons of "wiske" (Hamtramck spelled words as he pronounced them—with a French accent) would go to the company that finished first, four to the one that finished second—and the last company had to dig the ditch for the pickets. Hamtramck confided in his commander, Colonel Josiah Harmar, that he never intended that last insult; it was just a spur to get the job done. And it was done with dispatch. The contest began October 27, and the last blockhouse was finished January 8, 1787—a total of seventy-four days. The weather was so bad during that time, however, that Hamtramck calculated only thirty-three workdays.

On January 2, Hamtramck wrote to his commander, officially naming the fort then almost completed. Colonel Harmar expected Hamtramck to name it Fort Hamtramck; the fort at Marietta, after all, was named Fort Harmar. Instead, Hamtramck asked to name it after the inspector general of the colonial army, who had given Hamtramck his military training: General Frederick William von Steuben (or "Stuben," as Hamtramck spelled it).

The precarious nature of military pay, alluded to above, leads us to another Steubenville connection—and another story. Let's call it "The Mystery of the Missing Paper." It begins with the man who gave the Fort Steuben soldiers their pay—when they got it. The paymaster of the U.S. Army, Major Ekuries Beatty, had to deliver it personally and in coin. So once per month Major Beatty made the rounds of all the forts on the U.S. border, including, of course, the new Fort Steuben.

In fact, Beatty's army journal represents the earliest published description of Fort Steuben. And that's where the mystery begins. Major Beatty's official report of the new fort is quite detailed. When it was published in the first issue of the *Magazine of American History* (1877), we find the fort described on page 382 as "a square, with a large Block House on each corner, and picquets between each block house form the fort, much in this manner." After "this manner," there is nothing but a blank space. The sketch of the fort that must have followed this statement was missing when the editors transcribed Beatty's papers.

Where did that paper go? Well, we can presume it followed Beatty at first, so let's put on our detective hats and follow him. His last visit to Fort Steuben was in May 1787. The soldiers and surveyors were packing up for their next assignment. Beatty had been reassigned as well; this would be his last duty

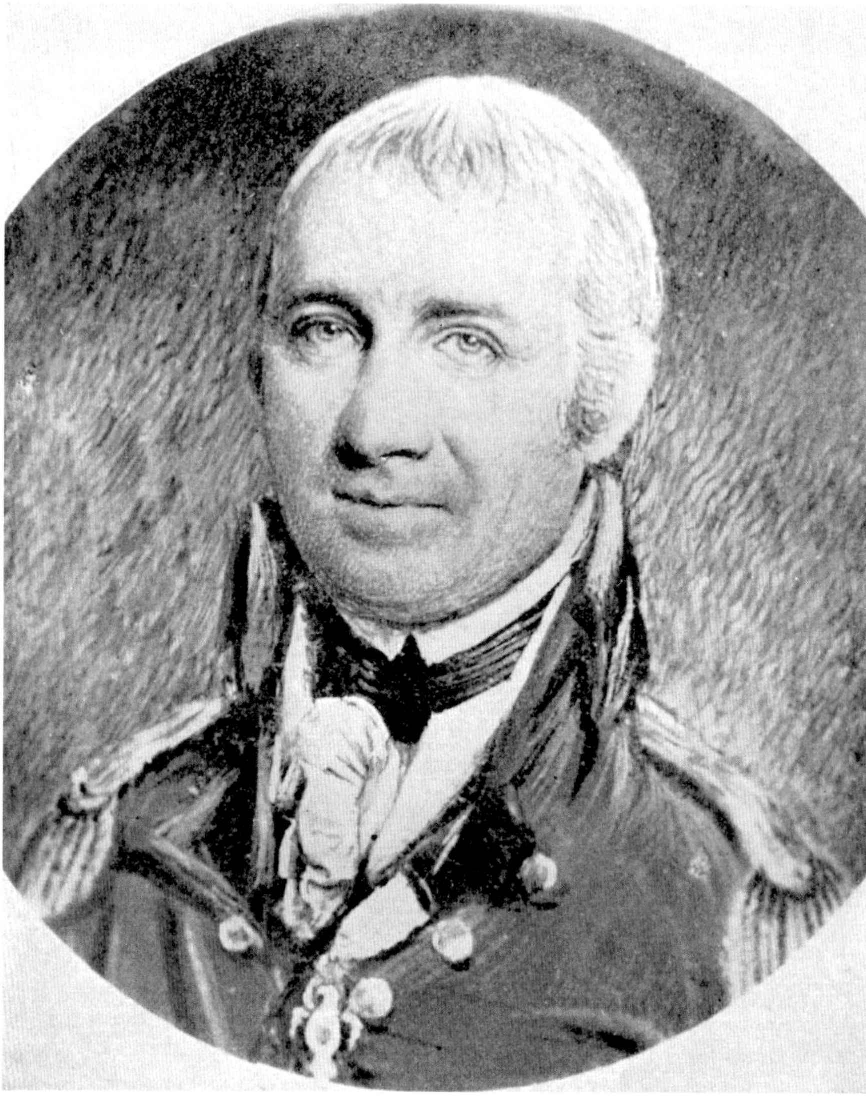

Major Ekuries Beatty, whose papers preserved the earliest sketch of Fort Steuben.
Archaeological and Historical Society of Ohio, Proceedings, *1898.*

as paymaster. He was an infantry officer again, assigned to Colonel Arthur St. Clair—namesake of Steubenville's downriver neighbor, St. Clairsville, Ohio. For the next four years, Major Beatty helped St. Clair build a number of forts on the Ohio frontier as confrontations with the Miami and the Shawnee became more and more inevitable.

Beatty's journal, presumably with the sketch of Fort Steuben, went with him as he helped build Fort Hamilton, north of present-day Cincinnati, in early October 1791, and then he immediately marched farther north (with the journal and the sketch) to build Fort Jefferson. When Fort Jefferson was completed at the end of October, St. Clair put it in Beatty's hands.

This assignment saved Beatty's life. It probably also saved the sketch. Had Major Beatty stayed with St. Clair, he would have experienced the biggest American military defeat since the Revolution. On November 4, 1791, combined forces of Miami under Michikinikwa (Little Turtle) and Shawnee under Weyapiersenwah (Blue Jacket) met St. Clair's 1,400 men and left 623 dead and 258 wounded. Many of the men who had built Fort Steuben were killed in this encounter.

We'll follow Major Beatty and his papers in a moment, but first, there's another Steubenville connection with this battle, a story in a story—though this one has recently turned out to be untrue. For more than a century, the leader of the Shawnee, known to the Americans as Blue Jacket, was thought to have been a captured American youth named Marmaduke van Swearingen. His father, Andrew van Swearingen, lived right across the river from Fort Steuben and was hired by Beatty to supply the soldiers with meat. In 1777, just a decade before Fort Steuben was built, fourteen-year-old Marmaduke was abducted by Shawnee, and years later when Blue Jacket emerged as a Shawnee leader, area legend identified him as the kidnapped Marmaduke.

This is a great story, but in 2006 that old spoilsport science came in and ruined it. This part of the story could be called *CSI: Steubenville*. DNA testing on Blue Jacket's remains were compared to the DNA of Van Swearingen descendants—many of whom still live in the upper Ohio Valley—and the results were conclusive: no connection between the two families. Blue Jacket was genetically Shawnee.

After his close brush with death, the ex-major (and his papers) returned to his Pennsylvania home. However, an old army buddy wrote to him about a business opportunity in Cumberland, New Jersey, so he moved there, married a local girl (Susannah Ewing) and settled down to raise a family. When his eldest son, Charles, grew up, he showed an aptitude for his grandfather's profession: the Presbyterian ministry. Ekuries owed his unusual name to his father's study of Biblical Greek: he coined the

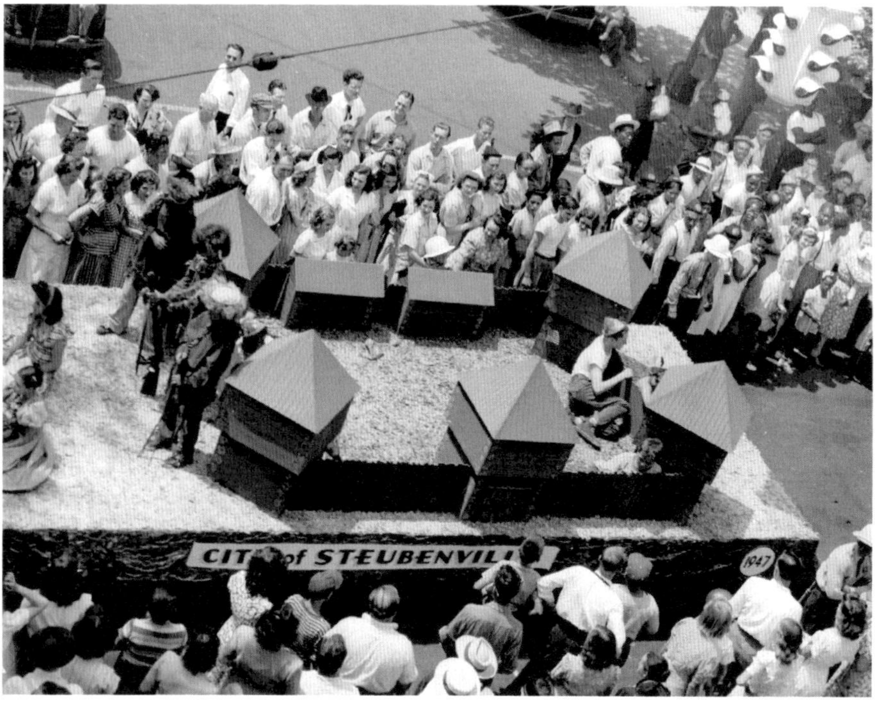

A float with a model of Fort Steuben in the Steubenville Bicentennial parade, 1947. *Ohio Collection, Schiappa Library.*

name from the Greek prefix *e-* ("out of" or "from") and *kyrie* ("the Lord"). Ekuries, however, did not live to see his son finish his doctorate at the Princeton Theological Seminary. He died in 1823—leaving his papers (including the sketch of the fort) to his son.

When he did finish the degree, however, and receive his ordination, Reverend Beatty asked to be assigned to the first church in America that became available. That turned out to be the Second Presbyterian Church in a little frontier town called Steubenville, Ohio. So Reverend Dr. Charles Clinton Beatty packed up all his books and papers—including his father's precious journal—and moved to Steubenville in 1825.

There is no indication that Reverend Beatty knew of his father's connection to his new hometown at the time that he moved, but we know that he did later. On September 14, 1850, Dr. Beatty wrote a letter to the editor of the Steubenville *Herald* correcting some misstatements in an article about Fort Steuben and mentioning the reporter's "seeing in my possession a Plan of the Fort, which I had found among my father's papers." So in 1850 the "missing" paper was in Steubenville.

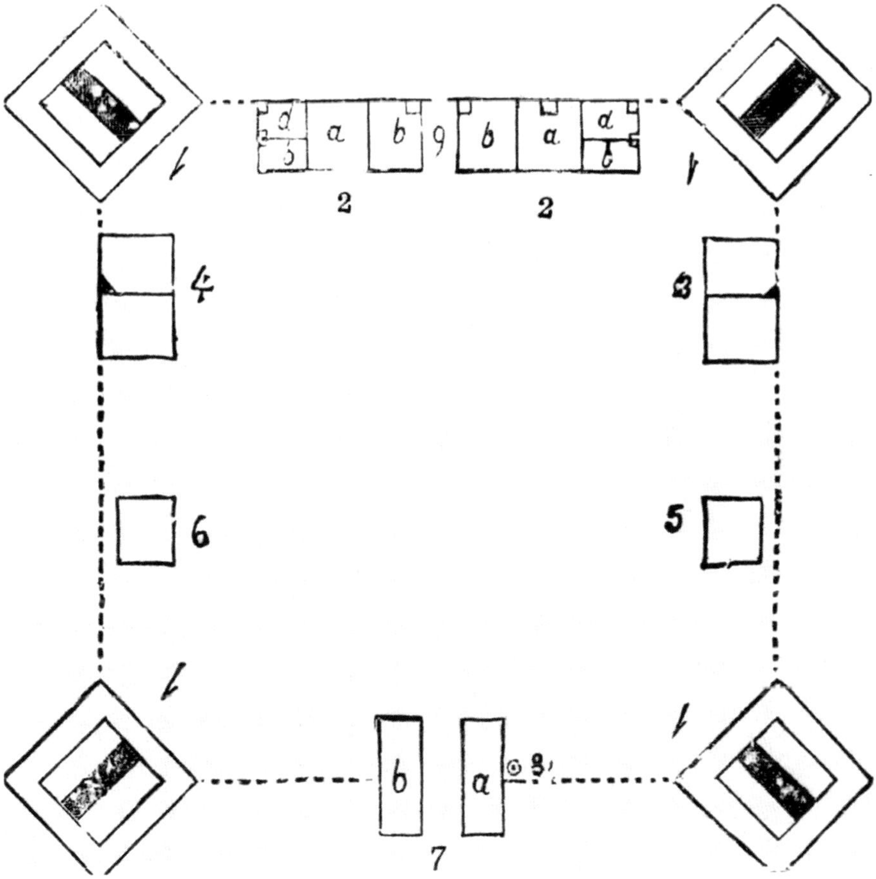

A sketch of Fort Steuben made in 1787. Centennial Souvenir of Steubenville and Jefferson County, O[hio], *1897.*

Then, a quarter century later, when Dr. Beatty loaned those papers to the editors of the *Magazine of American History*, he did not include the "Plan of the Fort," and the *Magazine* transcript read, "Here follows a blank in Mss." Did Dr. Beatty intentionally withhold it? Where was the missing paper in 1877?

Most likely, it was still with Beatty, because just four years later, on December 6, 1881, he published a facsimile in the *Herald*. He died the following year. Where did that original sketch go? No one knows. By surviving long enough for the rotogravure process to come to a small-town newspaper, the missing paper ensured that the vital image it carried would be preserved for future generations—in this very book, among other places.

The Founding

Though Fort Steuben figures large in the history of our town, it was only garrisoned for less than nine months—October 11, 1786, to May 30, 1787. After that, Hamtramck and the rest of the First American Regiment marched south and west, continuing the survey for a growing, land-hungry nation. It was here, in the upper Ohio Valley, that the first lands of the survey were sold in 1796. The Federal Land Offices that would open the West did not exist yet—the first one would be in Steubenville. The governor of the Northwest Territory, Winthrop Sargent—who had been at Fort Steuben a decade earlier—sold the land directly. Homesteaders could not buy the land directly from the government since federal regulations required land to be sold only in townships. Wealthy investors would buy whole town lots and sell them (at a profit) to homesteaders and developers.

A thirty-three-year-old entrepreneur named Bezaleel Wells saw his opportunity. His father, Alexander, had made a fortune across the river, arriving before the other settlers and setting up a gristmill, a sawmill and a smithy, as well as a distillery. Alexander chose wisely for the name of his third son. As he was building a town in the wilderness of Virginia (though in later border disputes it would become Washington County, Pennsylvania), he recalled the artificer who helped Moses build the tabernacle in the wilderness of Sinai—Bezale-el, "under the shadow of God." Our Bezaleel became a surveyor, not an artificer, but he did build whole towns—not just Steubenville, but also Canton, Ohio, and Wellsburg, West Virginia.

Bezaleel stood to inherit a large share of his father's fortune. But when the Ohio lands went up for sale, he knew that he couldn't wait. He asked for an advance on his inheritance, and the old man approved. On October 24, 1796, Wells, with his partner, Pittsburgh attorney James Ross, purchased eight sections of two townships—a total of 3,536½ acres. Wells, a skilled surveyor, laid out a town on what he thought was the best 200 acres of the lot and immediately advertized in the Pittsburgh papers for buyers. By August 25, 1797, nearly one hundred lots were sold (for an average of sixty dollars per lot) on the land that had been cleared by Castleman, Boley and Waddle and had been home to the soldiers of Fort Steuben. In honor of the fort, Wells named the new town Steubenville. With the proceeds from the lots, Wells and Ross bought even more sections and continued selling lots. In fact, they sold lots and lots of lots.

Though most of the lots outside that two-hundred-acre spread called Steubenville would become farms, Steubenville itself was commercial and residential from the start. John Ward bought a tract on the high ground

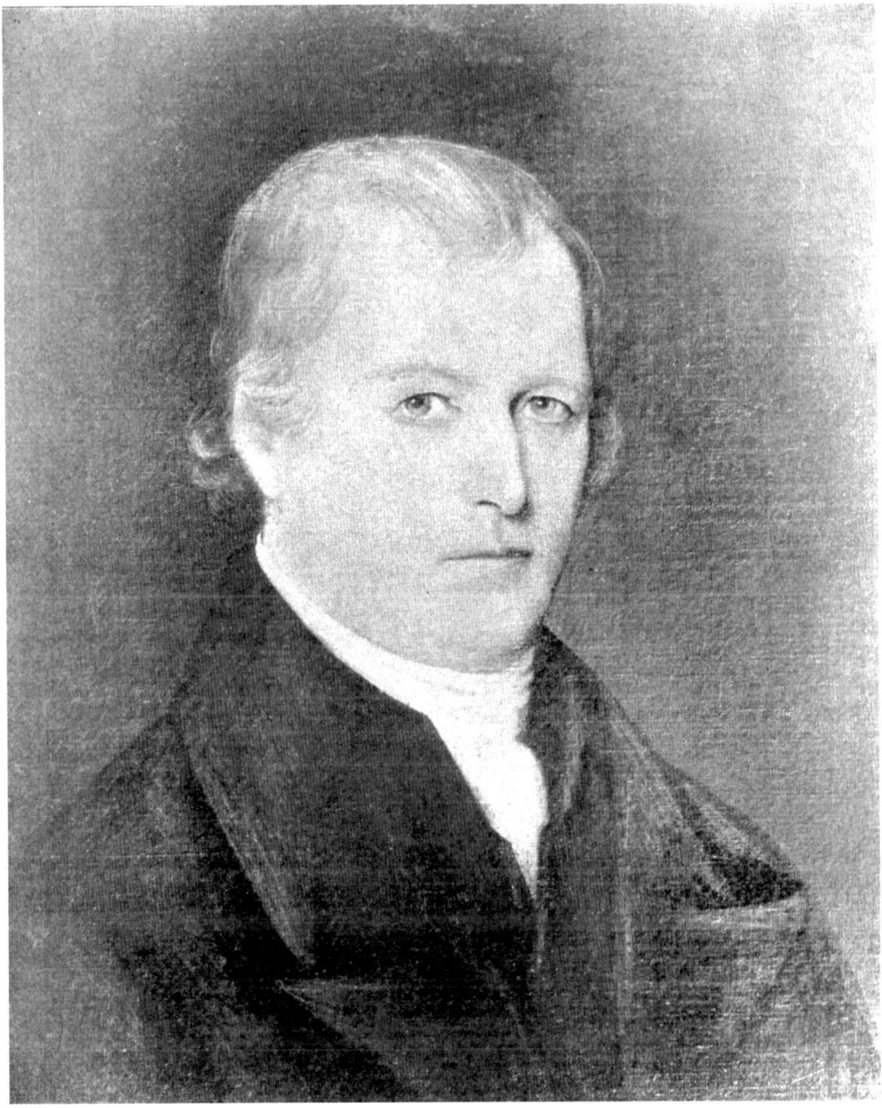

Bezaleel Wells, the Stein portrait, 1819—no longer extant but photographed by Filson in 1898. From *Archaeological and Historical Society of Ohio,* Proceedings, *1898.*

immediately above the wharf that Wells had built for the expected traffic of keelboats—Wells had, quite logically, named this High Street—and proceeded to build a brick hotel there. Just consider for a moment the sheer optimism of that act. Building a hotel where there was not yet a town. Yet it makes eminent sense. Speculators and homesteaders would need a place to stay while their homes were being built—and why not Ward's United States Hotel?

With equal audacity, Hans Wilson, in the summer of 1798, built the first store in the new town in the central area that Wells had already designated the town square. Wilson, an emigrant from Ireland, had already been well known on the frontier as a merchant without a store. With no stores in the wilderness, traders had to carry their own supplies or buy them from peddlers who carried astounding varieties of staple goods in their packs. Wilson was the best known of these wandering merchants in the upper Ohio, and now he had a permanent, square-log store to house his wares.

Wells had laid out the town modestly yet with room to grow. He followed the river for only four blocks, striking a road for the northern border and calling it "North Street" and one for the southern border called—well, you guessed it. The center boulevard was planned from the start as the commercial row and therefore named "Market Street," with a space offset for a public square—before there was even a public. That leaves only two more streets, one on either side of Market. Wells named them after the only U.S. presidents to date: Washington and Adams. Parallel to the river, Wells ran Water Street and then High Street, and then he numbered the remaining two, Third and Fourth. Just west of the new town, near the center of what is now Seventh Street, was the spring that had convinced Jacob Walker to build here thirty years earlier. Wells had logs hollowed out and buried them beneath the town, carrying fresh water to each of the sixteen blocks. In the next few years, four additional wells would be dug.

Very quickly, the market square became more than just a name. In the last two years of the eighteenth century, two more general stores moved into the square: John England's just west of Ward's and Samuel Hunter's on the southeast corner of Third and Market, right across from the new courthouse. Soon general stores were not general enough for the growing population. Moses Hale opened a dry goods store next door to Wilson's market, and next door to him Martin Andrews began selling hats and furs. If having a fur store sounds rather upscale for the new town, keep in mind that furs were still the number one trade good in the wilderness, and Steubenville represented the nearest market for many trappers. Far from a luxury, furs were the cheapest way to stay warm in Ohio on the eve of the nineteenth

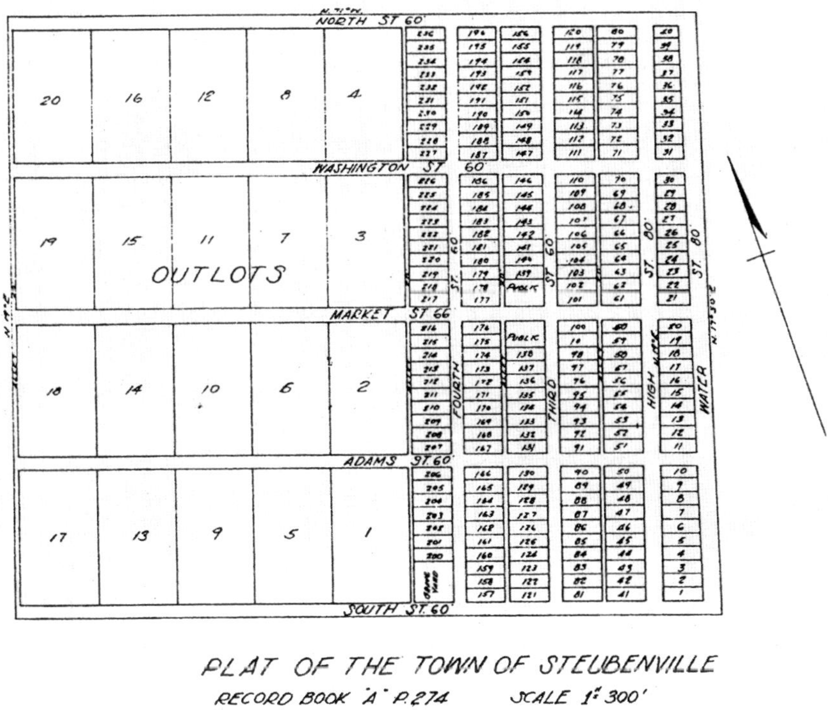

Plat of the original boundaries of Steubenville, as surveyed by Bezaleel Wells in 1797. *Ohio Collection, Schiappa Library.*

century. Except perhaps for whiskey, which was also traded freely in the market square.

First Federal Land Office

After about two years of this rapid growth and reinvestment, the government changed the rules for landowners. Farmers and merchants had resented being at the mercy of land barons, not all of whom were as honest and neighborly as Wells. So when the new citizens of the Ohio countryside finally gained a voice in Congress in 1799, their congressmen made their grievances known. Ohio was not yet a state, of course, but the entire Northwest Territory elected an Ohio boy, William Henry Harrison, to be its voice in Congress. Harrison put through a bill allowing citizens to buy, directly from the government, parcels of land as small as an acre, beginning at two dollars per acre. In addition, purchasers could use credit—half down, with four years to pay the remainder. A few good harvests could pay for a new farm.

The Harrison Land Act, signed into law April 15, 1800, necessitated, as is so often the case in American legislation, a whole new federal bureaucracy. If new landowners were to purchase plots directly from the government, they would need a government office in the new territory. So where else would the new nation locate its very first federal land office but the site of the very first federal land sale: Steubenville, Ohio. On May 10, 1800, Congress declared the Steubenville district the registration point of land sales in the Northwest Territory, and on May 12 President Adams named David Hoge, a Pennsylvania real estate agent, as recorder for the territories. Steubenville surveyor Zaccheus Biggs was named the first receiver. Biggs is better remembered in Harrison County as one of the two visionaries who laid out the town of Cadiz, Ohio, in 1804, though he lived the rest of his life in Steubenville, operating a ferry south of the town.

David Hoge was the face of the first Federal Land Office for most new landowners in Steubenville, from 1800 until the Steubenville district was dissolved in 1840. In 1801, Hoge built a square-log house on Third Street, just north of Market, which served as the land office until he moved in 1809. But at this point in the story, that little one-room structure took center stage and began having its own adventures. When Hoge moved across the street, the little log cabin moved with him. Twice, in fact. Then the "Little Home That Had No Home" was given more permanence. Steubenville was becoming an urban area—it was officially designated so in the 1830 U.S. Census. The architectural mark of urbanity was the three-story brick building. There was no room for a log cabin in such a place. Instead of moving the Little Home one more time, the builders took pity and, in 1828, simply bricked it up as part of a new building.

The Little Home was proud to be part of a big, sturdy new office building. Historians, and people who read children's stories, know that such pride will not last forever. The time would come when even the brightest new building would be left in the dust and shade of something newer and bigger and brighter. A century passed, then another dozen years, and in the spring of 1940 the three-story brick building itself was torn down. Imagine the excitement when, behind and under the bricks, the demolition crew found the squared timber of the Little Home That Had No Home. The patrons of Henry Roberts's barbershop across the street rushed out to look. Mr. Roberts knew right away what the beams were; his friend, George J. Barthold, was in the Jefferson County Historical Society and had told him the story of the

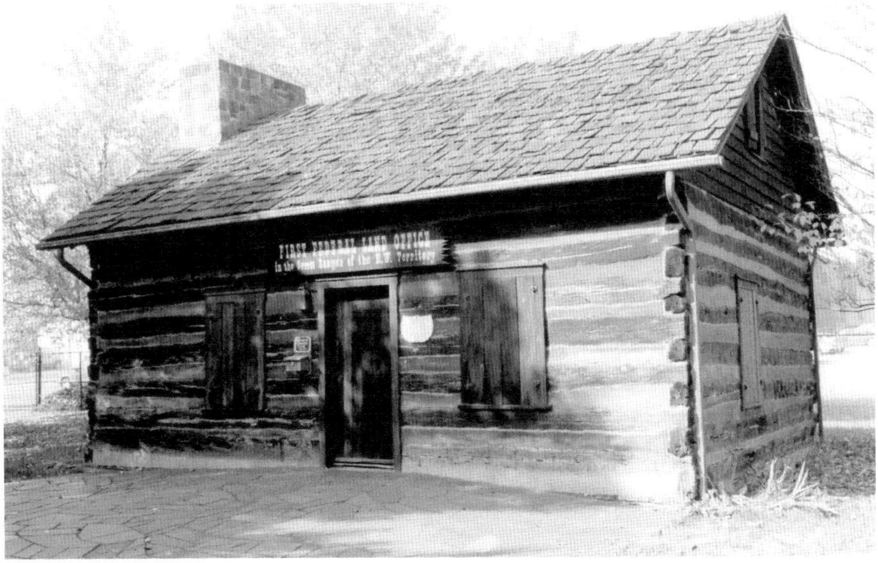

The first Federal Land Office—built in 1800 and dismantled and moved several times—still sports its original timbers. *Ohio Collection, Schiappa Library.*

Little Home. Roberts phoned Mr. Barthold immediately. "George! We've got to save our land office!"

So, that's just what they did. Barthold involved the president of the historical society, Market Street grocer Elza Scott, and the secretary of the Steubenville Automobile Club, Frank Thomas, and they immediately launched SOLO, "Save Our Land Office" (well, they didn't actually use that name, but that's what I would have called it). In the 1940s, historical preservation laws were not as strong as they are now, so they were unable to halt the demolition, but they were able to save the timbers, number them for reassembly and store them in a barn until they could find a home for the Little Home That Had No Home.

The committee was successful, collecting nickels and dimes from schoolchildren, a bit more from local businesses (the fact that Barthold was president of Miners & Mechanics Savings and Trust, one of the influential banking institutions in Steubenville, didn't hurt the cause) and finding available property, then just out of town but soon to be the "west end" of Steubenville. The Little Home finally had a place on Route 22, just opposite the county infirmary (the present-day site of Jefferson Community College). But the Little Home's travels were not yet over. In 1963, Route 22 had to be widened, and the land office was in the path of the new highway. Once again the Little Home had to find a new home. Luckily, there was a strip of land right on Route 7, a great showcase for passersby. At last the Little Home had a home.

For about twelve years. In 1976, Route 7 had to be redesigned to accommodate a new bridge. Again the Little Home was itinerant. Things looked hopeless for a while, but this time the Little Home's friends were not just local businessmen. The U.S. Department of the Interior announced that it would not award a contract for the bridge until the Little Home found a home. The Ohio Power Company off South Lake Erie Avenue took pity on the structure and gave it a temporary place, which became more permanent when Ohio Power itself moved, deeding the property to the city, which then turned it over to Fort Steuben—and to the Little Home That Now Had a Home (for now).

Now, is that how it really happened? Well, maybe. Despite the paper trail that always follows a federal agency, there have always been skeptics, ever since those beams were discovered behind the bricks in 1940. We know that David Hoge changed the location of the land office several times between 1801 and 1828, but it does not necessarily mean that he physically moved the building (though we know it was physically transported in 1941, 1963 and 1976). There is no proof that the beams uncovered in 1940 came from the land office built in 1801. However, we know that they were bricked over in 1828 and were already old then—so the attractive story of the Little Home That Had No Home turns out to be as likely as any.

PART II

What Granddad Did: Pioneer Industries

Sheep, Steam and Jeans

As the seat of Jefferson County and headquarters of its own land district, Steubenville grew quickly in the early nineteenth century. An English travel writer in 1806 spoke of 160 homes in the city proper. Land sales slowed during the War of 1812 (to which Jefferson County contributed fourteen companies of men, or 1,065 soldiers), but resumed with the peace in 1814. When young Eli McFeely arrived by keelboat in October of that year, he estimated the population at 800 or 900 residents.

Bezaleel Wells knew that the key to Steubenville's prosperity was the river, both for transport and for power. His father, Alexander Wells, had made his fortune by using the Pennsylvania creeks to power his gristmills, centering his other businesses around them. Wells built his own gristmill in Steubenville in 1802, though Steubenville entrepreneurs had preceded him in other industries: Benjamin Doyle's tannery in 1798 and P. Snyder's distillery in 1800. In 1807, Arthur Phillips set up a blacksmith shop, which would become an iron foundry, the first step in a long history of metallurgy in Steubenville. Much of the capital for these businesses came from Wells's continued land sales—and many of those sales were in turn made possible with mortgage loans from Wells. In light of this investment activity, Wells opened the First Bank of Steubenville in 1808.

In the twentieth century, locals referred to the upper Ohio Valley—Columbia, Jefferson and Belmont Counties, at least, and the northern panhandle of West Virginia—as "Steel Valley." A century earlier, though, the most prosperous industry in Steubenville was wool. Steel was so vital in building late nineteenth- and early twentieth-century America that it is easy for us to overlook the importance of the first American woolen mills. Economically, they can be considered a second American Revolution. Thomas Jefferson's complaint in the Declaration of Independence about England's George III "cutting off our Trade with all parts of the world" was particularly pointed in terms of industrialization. The Crown wanted the American colonies to be client states, supplying raw materials to the world's first industrialized nation, England, making it the first industrial monopoly. Wells's construction of one of the first woolen mills in the new nation changed all that. Another factor was the sheep themselves.

Bezaleel Wells's prize sheep were the first key to Steubenville becoming the knit-wool capital. In 1811, when William Jarvis returned to the United States as ambassador to Portugal, he brought with him some Spanish Merino sheep, considered to bear the finest and softest wool of any sheep. Steubenville sheep of the time bore wool at 6 percent of body weight; Jarvis's Merinos bore twice that (while eating the same amount of feed). Wells bought several Merinos from Jarvis, grazing them near Canton and wintering them at his estate south of Steubenville. Since the gestation period of sheep is five months, and since ewes can be bred as early as seven months, Wells's flock grew quickly. By 1824 he had 5,500 head.

The second key to Steubenville's woolen trade was the development of steam power. In the fall of 1814, Wells, his old partner James Ross, Samuel Patterson and Henry Baldwin built a three-story brick factory to the north of the rapidly expanding town, accessible to Market Street, at what is now Seventh. The following spring he outfitted it with a steam engine that powered carding, rolling, drawing, knapping, spinning and, eventually, even shearing machines. Three jennies with a total of 160 spindles produced large quantities of fine wool thread. Similar facilities existed in New England at that time, but the Steubenville operation introduced an innovation. Two master hand loom weavers, John Arthurs and Robert Semple, were engaged to devise a loom driven by the steam engine. Their experiments succeeded, and the first broadcloth made by steam power came from Steubenville and went out, via the Ohio River, to the world.

The third key to the wool empire in Steubenville was the availability of cheap fuel to produce that steam power. Steubenville sat on one of the richest deposits of mineral coal in the world—in the early days it was so close to the surface that the first residents simply dug it out by hand. That's a story in itself, but we'll get to that later.

Wells did not keep the bounty of Merino wool to himself. The bloodlines of his sheep spread throughout the hills of Jefferson County. When financial difficulties put an end to the Wells wool fortunes in 1830—his entire

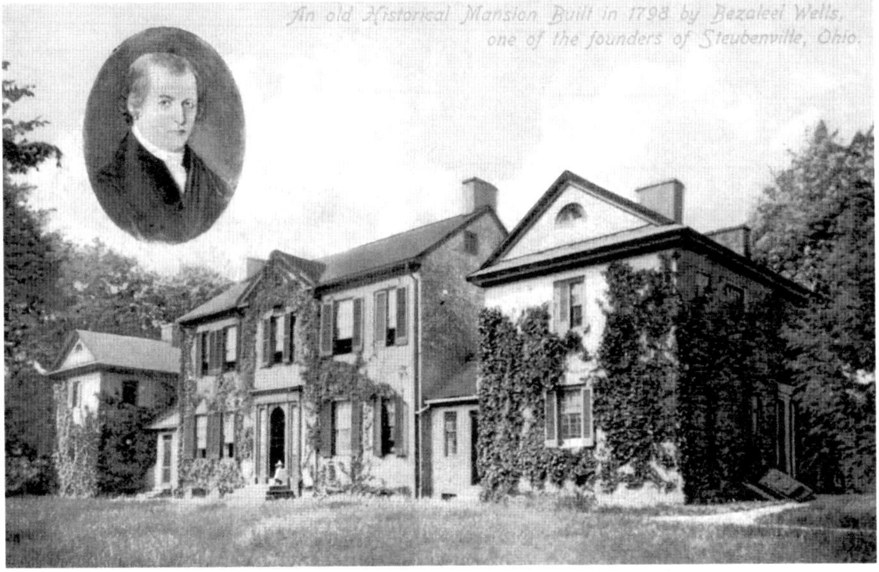

The Grove, a mansion built by Bezaleel Wells in 1798. *Ohio Collection, Schiappa Library.*

flock and factory had to be sold when his loans were called by the federal government—the wool trade was too well established in Steubenville to go away. In 1832, James H. Blinn bought the factory, modernized the machinery and went into business making woolen and cotton pants.

The farmers and workmen who made up Blinn's clientele wanted sturdy work pants, so Blinn used a denim design that had first seen use in the Genoan navy in the sixteenth century, dyed Genoan blue—*bleu Genes*—hence their popular American name, "blue jeans." Blinn was certainly not the first American to make blue jeans, but he was doing so more than twenty years before Levi Strauss, who made that most American of clothing style for western miners in 1855. By that time so many blue jeans were being exported from Steubenville that the portion of the city south of Washington and west of Fifth became an enclave of weavers, known as "Jeans Town."

By 1835, there were six woolen mills and three cotton factories in Steubenville. Larimore, Culp & Co.'s cotton works opened in 1824 on Adams and Water and William Gwynn's (Arkwright Cotton Factory) in 1826 on Washington and Water, both able to load directly onto flatboats moored at the riverbank. James Wallace's cotton mill stood at the top of Market Street—just west of Seventh, then the outskirts of town. Armstrong and Northrop had their jeans works on South Seventh. The woolen mills of Robert C. Peters on South Fifth were nicknamed "Golgotha" ("place

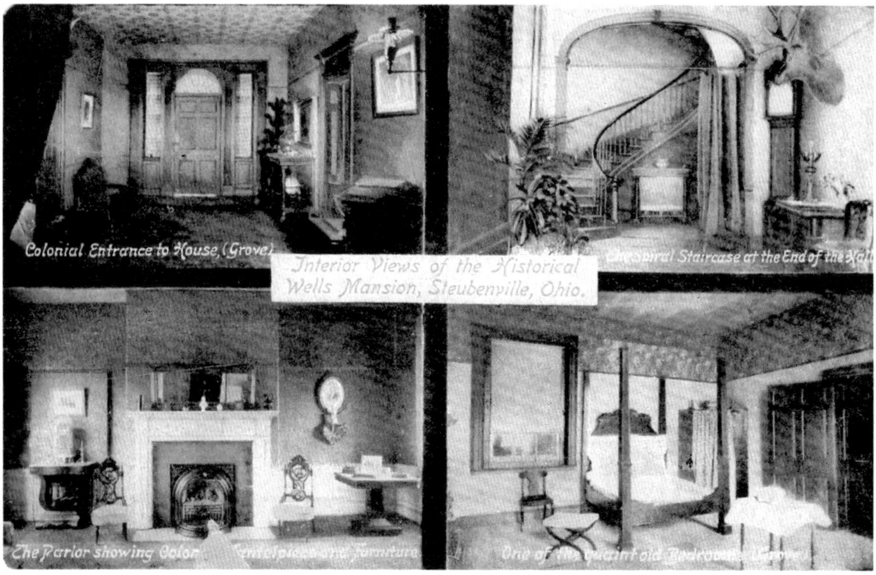

Interior views of the Wells mansion, from an old postcard. *Ohio Collection, Schiappa Library.*

of skulls") because they stood opposite the city graveyard. A letter to the Steubenville *Herald* mentions Woolcott's factory producing "considerably more" than 200,000 pounds of wool per year in Steubenville, but no further record of that company has survived. McDowell's on Water Street, the Rockville factory on the west end of South Street and the Franklin factory on Seventh Street all produced wool cloth, mostly exported to New Orleans.

FROM COAL VALLEY TO STEEL VALLEY

The role of Steubenville coal in the city's wool industry was incidental: the factories could produce steam power almost as easily by burning wood, and until the middle of the nineteenth century, that's just what they did. But coal was absolutely vital for the development of the iron and steel industries here.

Wells and Ross were aware of the coal deposits in the area even in 1796 as they bought the land that would become Steubenville. Coal seams were visible wherever creeks and streams cut into hillsides, and in 1810 Bezaleel Wells began drift mining all of his unsold lots that showed black. Drift mining is a method of cutting horizontally into a hill, rather than sinking a shaft. Wells began below the seams and cut up into them, so that gravity would bring the coal down for him. Coal was not yet vital as a fuel, though; Wells sold the mines to John Permar and James Odbert, who ran the small operation until 1816.

Drift mining continued to be profitable right into the middle of the century, and the town leaders felt that production would be sufficient to supply the 1,500 bushels per day needed to feed the rolling mills that Steubenville businessmen wanted. The puff piece on the town's businesses that appears in the 1850 Steubenville directory was quite explicit:

> *The advantages for manufacturing Iron at this place, are so great, that it is a matter of surprise, that this enterprise has not been carried out long since. There are beautiful Rolling Mill sites in the vicinity of this town, that can be furnished with a superior quality of coal for the small sum of 1¾ cents per bushel: whereas many companies at this time, successfully engaged in this business at other points, are paying from 3½ to 4½ cents per bushel.*

The type of deep-shaft mining pursued in Europe at the time did not seem practical to the miners in Steubenville—or perhaps they just didn't know how to go about it. In 1829, Adam Wise, who a decade earlier had been the engineer on the maiden voyage of the steamship *Bezaleel Wells* (but that story is coming up), was drilling for water when he found a coal vein 11 feet thick at a depth of 225 feet.

No one in Steubenville, however, had any experience in underground mining, so no coal came out of this hole until nearly thirty years later and then not enough to satisfy the speculators, James Wallace and James Warner, both prosperous wool merchants. In 1859, they sold the mine and equipment to another group of Steubenville investors—Reynolds, Borland and Manful—who erected what would be, for more than a century, a distinctive icon of Steubenville: the wooden coal tipple over the mine that would soon be known as "the High Shaft."

In 1865, the company passed to its third group of owners. James Wallace, one of the original owners, returned to the business, along with James Blinn, the man who had bought Steubenville's first wool factory from Wells, as well as attorney George W. McCook and banker Robert Sherrard. Taking over the mine, these four incorporated the Steubenville Coal and Mining Company in 1865, which pulled coal from beneath the city of Steubenville, to depths up to nine hundred feet, until 1952. Mining was not halted because the vein had been played out—estimates at the time suggested that coal could be removed at then current rates (seventy-five tons a day) for another thirty-five years. Instead, modern mining equipment could not operate in

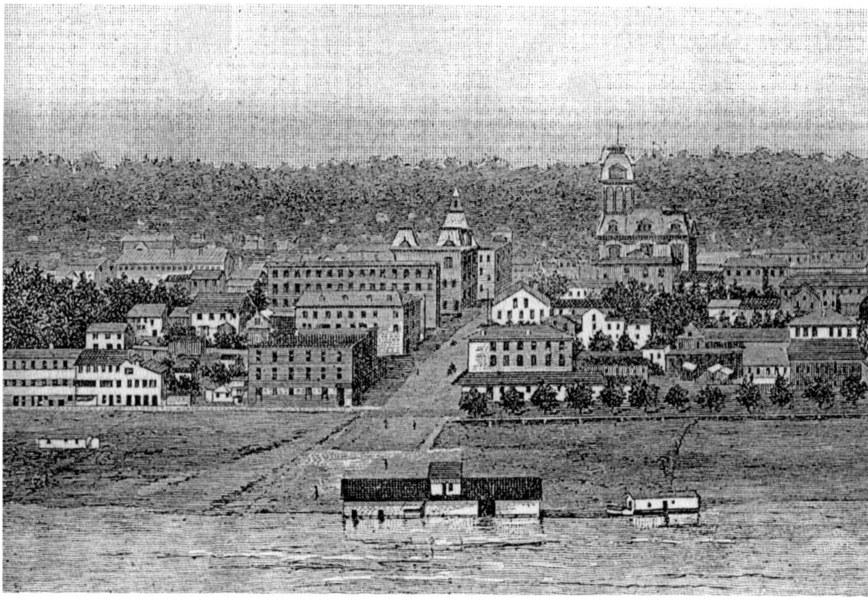

Steubenville's Market Street wharf looking from the river, 1886. The Jefferson County Courthouse dominates the background, right. *Ohio Collection, Schiappa Library.*

the one-hundred-year-old design of this mine. And so a great Steubenville tradition came to an end.

The recognizable shape of the coal tipple—a peaked wooden structure covering a bucket that loaded coal onto railroad cars—remained at the High Shaft on the highest point of Market Street for another dozen years after the mining halted, washing and separating coal already mined. In 1964, it was torn down.

The purpose of coal mining in Steubenville, from the 1850s onward, was to serve iron and steel production in the city. Yes, I can say "city" now, because the rapid expansion of Steubenville led to its incorporation as a city in 1851. In 1830, the population of Steubenville had been 2,937, placing it among the one hundred top urban areas in the United States (at no. 85, only 157 people behind Mobile, Alabama—and 314 ahead of Annapolis, Maryland). By 1850, the Steubenville population had more than doubled in size at 6,140. Business was booming, and industrialists could count on a strong workforce for heavy industry.

In one sense, ironwork had been a part of every village since ancient times. Iron may have been smelted in West Africa as early as 1200 BCE, and by the middle ages in Europe, every town had a smithy. A town the size of Steubenville had many, the largest right by the river on Market; it was damaged when a cyclone touched down in Steubenville in 1820. But the mass production of iron and steel in the city would wait until the middle of the nineteenth century. In Steubenville there were sporadic developments beyond the local blacksmiths and ferriers: nail-cutting, an industry closely associated with nearby Wheeling, began in 1811 in Steubenville at the shop of the Thompson brothers, Andrew and Robert. The first iron foundry, however, was established by blacksmith Arthur M. Phillips in 1816. He built his forges right on the river between Washington and North Streets, just upriver from the foot of the present-day Veterans Memorial Bridge. This allowed him to unload ore from keelboats and float his end product to market the same way. It also put Phillips in a position to get in on the ground floor of the new steamboat industry, as we shall see in the next section.

In the 1830s, the Phillips foundry was purchased by James Means, and Means's sons continued to operate it to the end of the century. But it would not long remain the only ironworks in Steubenville. In January 1845, an Irish immigrant named William L. Sharp opened an ironmonger's shop on Fourth Street in Steubenville (the city directory listed him as a "tinner"). His main trade was selling prefabricated iron and tin goods, but in those days an ironmongery—then the equivalent of a hardware store—was expected to repair, and sometimes make to order, any kind of iron implement.

Sharp was up to the task. When his parents died in 1823, he had apprenticed to a Quaker metalworker in Philadelphia. His coal cooking stoves became so popular in Steubenville that Sharp began marketing them nationally in the summer of 1845. Part of his success in Jefferson County is no doubt attributable to the fact that he gladly accepted barter goods for his stoves at a time when Ohio's economy was increasingly cash-only. Sharp would accumulate whole herds made up of cows traded for stoves; when the herd got too big, Sharp would stage some of the largest cattle drives in the East, moving across Pennsylvania to the Philadelphia stockyards, where he traded them for pig iron to make more stoves.

In 1847, Sharp moved his operation to the experimental mine shaft at Fifth and Market Streets, which was yet to produce any coal. There he established the Ohio Foundry, which would within a decade stimulate the mine to produce the foundry's fuel. It was with this company that Sharp put into practice three principles of his old Quaker master. The first was simply his craft, making superior iron products. The other two were religious. Although Sharp did not himself become a Quaker, two of his master's religious principles would directly affect the business of the Ohio Foundry in Steubenville: pacifism and an abhorrence of slavery. Sharp used Ohio Foundry barges and delivery wagons to smuggle escaped slaves on the

Underground Railroad. As for pacifism, Sharp turned down four years of lucrative contracts to produce cannonballs for the Union army.

As in so many families, however, the Civil War divided generations in the Sharp family. William stood by his pacifist principles, and two of his sons, Samuel and Henry, stood by their father. They were too young to enlist in any case; when they came of age, both became ministers. Their oldest brother, George, joined the infantry in his eighteenth year. Unlike most new recruits, he had already seen battle after a fashion, chasing after Morgan's Raiders just west of Steubenville. That story has been told repeatedly in local books, though, and it doesn't really touch Steubenville directly, so we'll save it for another time.

Immediately after the war, George joined the firm, now called Sharp & Son (though in the twentieth century the family somehow acquired an "e" in its name). Four generations of Sharp(e)s led the company well into the twentieth century. When the founder, William, died in 1902, his son, George, became president until 1926, when he died and his son, Alexander, took over.

The Ohio Foundry was just one of the ironworks of nineteenth-century Steubenville. In 1856, Frazier, Kilgore & Co. began making iron bars and nails south of the city. In 1859, a group of nearly a dozen Steubenville investors bought the works and operated it under the name of the two biggest partners, Spalding, Woodward & Co.

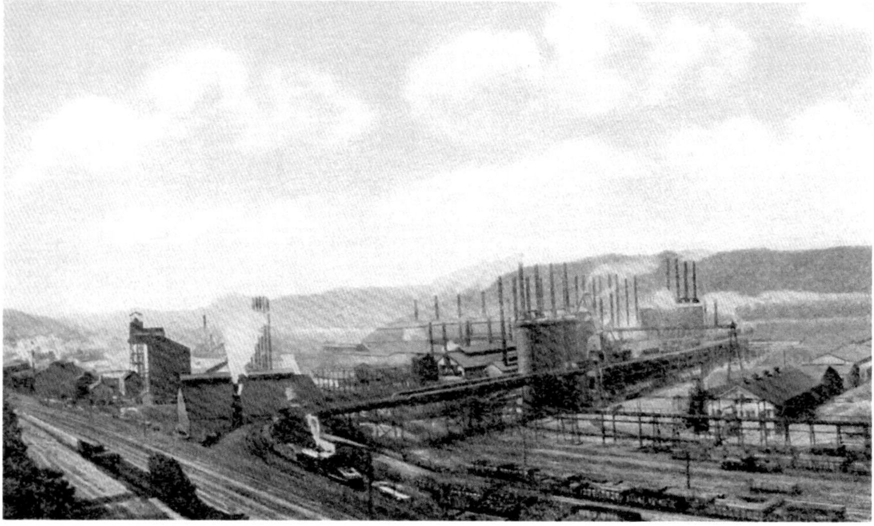

La Belle Ironworks in 1907. *Ohio Collection, Schiappa Library.*

Their timing was perfect. The Civil War came along just as their business was building up, and they took up the war contracts that Sharp had refused, adding two blast furnaces and a coke oven and sinking their own coal shaft. After the war, they continued to grow, and in 1882 they reincorporated as the Jefferson Ironworks Company. They shipped directly from the river opposite their plant, and three railroad companies ran tracks to service the factory.

La Belle Ironworks of Wheeling bought the Steubenville plant in 1890 and was in turn bought in 1920 by Wheeling Steel Corporation. This consolidation was the beginning of a large expansion after the First World War. War contracts had built up the steel industry, and workers made great sacrifices for the war effort. But with the armistice, labor organizers saw their chance to unionize an entire industry. The result was the Great Steel Strike of 1919, which shut down steel production in Steubenville, and in the rest of the country, from September 22, 1919, to January 8, 1920. It also, of course, stopped salaries. Workers nationwide lost $112 million, but when the smoke cleared, the entire steel industry was unionized, companies merged and business boomed.

The Booze Biz

America's constantly changing attitudes toward alcohol can be seen in the fortunes of Steubenville's own brewing and distilling industries. Distilling was always a cottage industry in Steubenville during its brief flourishing in the first two decades of the nineteenth century. Michael Roberts of Steubenville made and sold stills to local farmers up and down the Ohio circa 1800, and whiskey and corn liquor were marketed like any other commodity in Steubenville and downriver. Commercial beer breweries were active in Steubenville long before the mid-1800s German immigration associated with urban breweries in America.

Indeed, beer had been an important part of American life long before the Revolution. In Steubenville the first commercial brewer, according to historian Joseph P. Doyle, was a man named Dunlop, who began producing pale ales, strong beer and "table beer" in 1815 at his North Third Street brewery. "Table beer" was the ancestor of today's so-called nonalcoholic beer (which can contain up to 0.5 percent alcohol); its alcohol content was about 1.5 percent, while even modern "light" beers contain over 4 percent. This moment in Steubenville brewing history finds breweries consonant with "family values"—table beer with alcohol contents that low suggests beer intended to be served with food and as food.

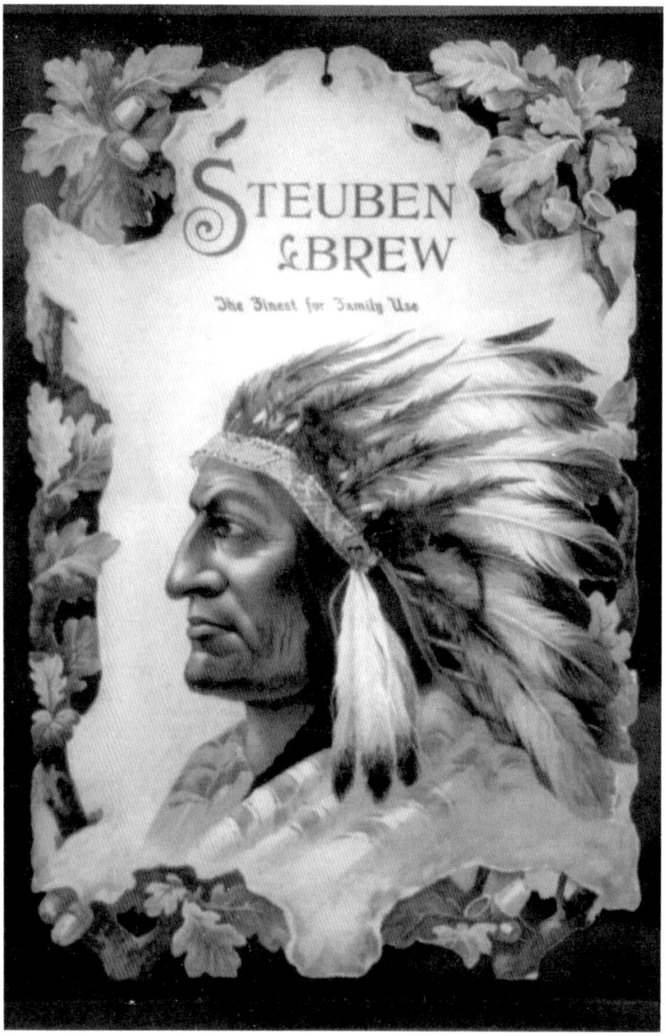

Store poster promoting Steuben Brew, 1907. *Photo courtesy of Donald E. Wild, Ohio Collection, Schiappa Library.*

As early as 1816, Dunlop was advertising his product in New Orleans, where his barrels arrived on flatboats: "New Orleans Market / STRONG ALE / TABLE BEER / May be had at the Steubenville Brewery, at $3.50 per barrel, and $1.75 per half barrel. / Steubenville, November 4, 1816." By 1818, Dunlop's production was bought out by Charles H. Leiblin, and the following year a rival brewery run by Alexander Armstrong appeared on Water Street near Washington. One of Leiblin's brewers, Joseph Basler, bought Armstrong's operation in the 1830s, and he and his sons continued brewing until well after the Civil War.

According to beer historian Carl H. Miller in a February 26, 1996 *Herald Star* article, the beers of these early breweries would not be the German-style lagers that are most common in the American market today, but rather English-style ales, porters and stouts. Steubenville's most famous brewers, however, two German-born Johanns, would introduce lagers to Steubenville. The Prussian Baron von Steuben, who liked his lager, would have been proud.

By the middle of the 1800s, German immigrants in Steubenville became a major part of the city's culture. By the 1880s, there was a German-language newspaper in the city, the *Steubenville Germania*, and two popular German brass bands. The city's biggest celebration prior to its centennial in 1897 was the 1890 *Steubenfeier*, though it is not remembered in the English-language histories. *Steubenfeier*, or "Steuben-celebration," was a German-American celebration of the city's connection with its German namesake, Baron von Steuben. It was filled with German music, German food and locally brewed German lager.

The first Johann, the first German immigrant to brew lager in Steubenville, was John C. Butte, who arrived in Steubenville in 1860 and built a lager brewery on Adams Street, which he simply called the City Brewery. Cold aging is key to a lager's taste, so Butte dug one-hundred-foot-deep cellars, which he packed with ice. Cold storage was a major Steubenville industry in the 1800s—ice ponds were cut into blocks and stored in cellars packed with insulating sawdust. Butte's cellars were insulated enough to keep the ice frozen—and the lager cold—all summer.

The second Johann, John Buehler, came long after Butte had retired and sold the business. But when Buehler bought the City Brewery in 1895, artificial refrigeration technology had revolutionized the lager cold-brewing process. Buehler completely modernized the plant, adding electric refrigeration in 1898 and a separate power plant to run it in 1901. Buehler produced three brand names, City Brew, Pale American and Select, and in 1907 he introduced Steuben Brew.

The timing could not have been worse. The family-friendly beer ethic of the "table beer" era was gone. While many Americans hoped to draw a distinction between beer and wines and distilled "hard" liquor in the shadow of the Women's Christian Temperance Union (which, as Mark Twain observed, was temperate in everything but its temperance), the WCTU refused to make such allowances and included beer in its war on demon rum. The Eighteenth Amendment, and its enforcing legislation the Volstead Act, would not be ratified until 1919. But the State of Ohio had its own prohibition in 1908—less than a year after the introduction of Steuben Brew.

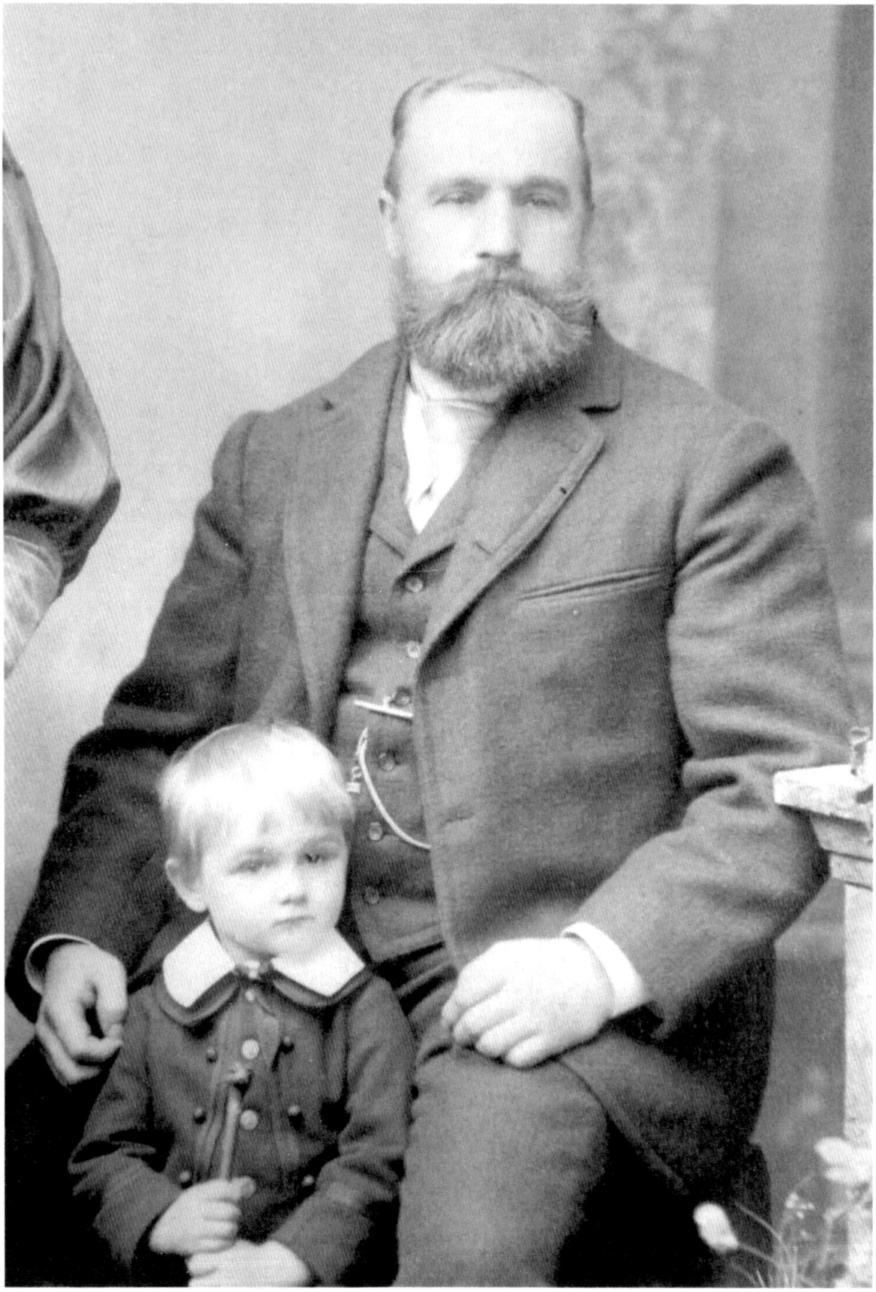

Steubenville brewmeister John Buehler and his son, Charles, who later took over his father's trade. *Ohio Collection, Schiappa Library.*

Actually, the Ohio law simply left alcohol sales and consumption laws up to the local communities, and Jefferson County voted to be dry. In this foretaste of Prohibition, a decade early, compliance followed exactly the same pattern as Prohibition in the 1920s. That is, otherwise law-abiding citizens ignored this one law and found ways to buy, sell and consume illegal beverages on the sly. Speakeasies sprang up before there was a word for them, and most criminal activity was tied in some way with the sale of alcohol.

Consequently, although Buehler could legally sell his lager outside of Jefferson County, overzealous lawmen assumed that finding bottles of Steuben Brew or Pale American in the city limits proved that Buehler was breaking the law. Whether he was guilty or not, Buehler was forced to halt production in 1910 to avoid lawsuit. In 1912, Jefferson County repealed the law, and Buehler reopened the business with his son, Charles T. Buehler. National Prohibition six years later, however, closed beer production for good.

Charles kept the family business going (just barely) through Prohibition by converting the plant to making malt syrup, leasing it to a company in Peoria. When the home office closed down the Steubenville operation, Charles rode the corporate ladder. When his Peoria company merged with Pabst, Charles became a corporate executive of one of the biggest beer makers in American brewing history.

The misfortunes of the Buehler family in responding to changing attitudes toward liquor were skillfully avoided by B.W. Mettenberger. He came of age in the liquor business, and even when he tried to get into other lines of work, he found himself squeezed out by other businessmen with a distaste for anyone associated with the trade. In 1877, at the age of seventeen, Mettenberger began as a clerk for a liquor wholesaler simply because he could not find any other job. Over the next few years, he worked a number of odd jobs but always seemed to end up in the booze biz, finally delivering beer for Schnorrenberg's bottling company.

Two boons came from this job: a knowledge of the livery trade, from managing the horses for beer deliveries, and a conviction that he could run the business better than Schnorrenberg, who paid more attention to his other business, publishing the *Steubenville Germania*. Agreeing with the younger man, Schnorrenberg helped him obtain a loan for $3,800 to buy the business. Mettenberger paid off the loan in eight months, and found himself in 1881, at the age of twenty-one, owner and proprietor of the City Bottling House and its stable of delivery horses.

Once again Mettenberger's natural business instincts took over. Recognizing that beer deliveries took up only a small fraction of the horses'

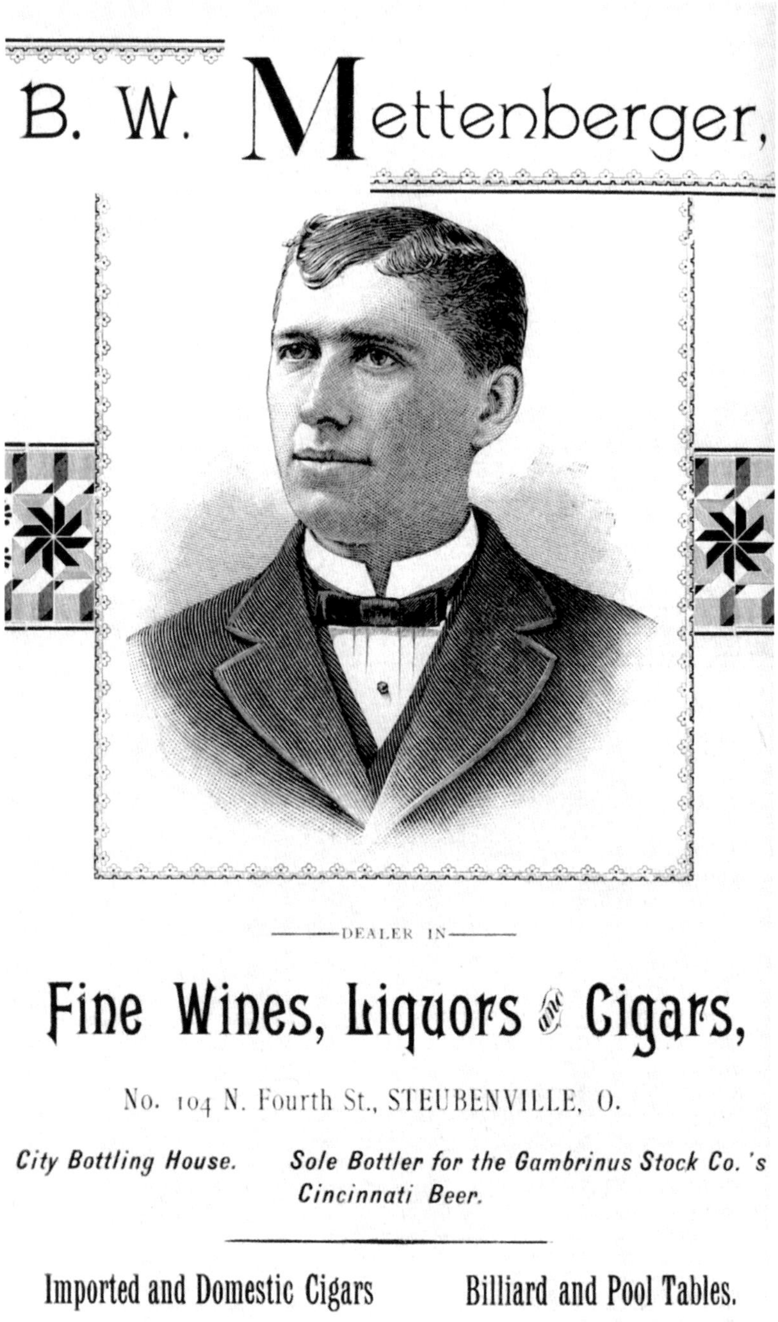

Beer bottler B.W. Mettenberger tried for a more exclusive clientele in 1892 but was forced out of the liquor business in 1902. Steubenville City Directory 1892–93. *Schiappa Library copy.*

available energy, he reasoned that he could operate the delivery team as a livery stable. Some of the most lucrative clients for livery stables were the funeral homes, who wanted to hire fine carriages for funeral processions. And so, by working closely with Steubenville's top funeral directors, Mettenberger picked up a third trade.

In the meantime, Mettenberger spruced up his image in Steubenville's liquor trade. While still selling and bottling beer, he courted a more upscale clientele in the 1890s by dealing in fine imported wines and cigars. But it was all in vain. To the WCTU types, any tincture of an alcoholic beverage left a permanent mark on a businessman's character, and polite people did not trade with a dealer in that commodity. Gloves that touch liquor shall never touch my horseflesh. The funeral directors might have been growing chummy with Mettenberger, but they had to deal more closely with Steubenville's clergymen, who were becoming increasingly embroiled in the uncompromising temperance movement. Thus, one day the entire Steubenville funeral industry stopped dealing with Mettenberger.

Blacklisted, frozen out of the livery business, Mettenberger at first seemed to cave in to the pressure when he sold his liquor business in 1902. Then, however, he struck back at the funeral businesses that had snubbed him by going into competition with them. He combined his livery business with a successful funeral home that took a good deal of business away from the men who had tried to ruin his livelihood.

Steubenville Steamships

The notion of Steubenville having a world market so early in its development is no exaggeration. Keelboat packets regularly docked at Steubenville on their way to New Orleans and from there to the European market. But soon the secret of Steubenville's woolen triumphs would be applied to river transportation. The histories of the steamboat that list Robert Fulton's 1811 launch of the first continuous passenger steamboat line in Pittsburgh, with New Orleans as its final destination, usually fail to mention that its first port of call was Steubenville, Ohio, where the *New Orleans* docked for the night of its maiden voyage (March 18).

Excited by the advent of commercial steamboat travel—the first steamship to make the return trip from New Orleans passed Steubenville in 1815—the merchants of Steubenville were eager to join the new industry. In 1819, iron maker Arthur M. Phillips, whose early foundry is described in the previous section, received an order for a steamship engine and boiler for the steamboat *Mercury*, prompting the simple but provocative question: why should we export our own technology to the betterment of other cities?

Shipwright Elijah Murray responded by building a boatyard right next to the Phillips foundry, and by the following spring, the yard had produced its first steamboat, a 126-ton side-wheeler that Murray, with hometown pride, named the *Bezaleel Wells*. The chimney was made of brick by Steubenville mason Ambrose Shaw, but a collision with the shore sent it toppling, and it had to be replaced by a conventional iron smokestack. The next trip to Pittsburgh saw a top speed of the *Wells* at about three miles an hour. That may seem frightfully slow to us, but Pittsburgh is upstream from Steubenville, and even at that pace the *Wells* left keelboats far behind. The progress was still painfully slow, however, as the force pump that fed water to the boiler broke, and the well-dressed passengers were obliged to help fill it.

Though the *Wells* continued in operation for another two years in Louisville, the best work of Murray's boatyard was yet to come. Yet Steubenville craftsmen were still in a sense exporting their technology, for though they produced nine boats in the next decade—a respectable rate at that time—none of them serviced the Steubenville trade. The *Mechanic* (1820) and the *Aurora* (1820) went to Wheeling; the *Superior* (1822) and the *Steubenville* (1823) to New Orleans; the *Robert Thompson* (1821), *Niagara* (1829) and the *Lady Byron* (1830) to Pittsburgh; the *Congress* (1822) to Louisville; and the *Tallyho* (1830) to Nashville.

That would change, however, with Steubenville river captain George A. Dohrman. Dohrman had been the original pilot on the *Robert Thompson*, reportedly the first steamboat with a Lancashire or double-flue boiler, reducing the amount of time required to build up a head of steam. His brother, Peter, had been the pilot on that ship, but when George left the river to run a mail coach to Wheeling, Peter advanced to captain and George suggested that the mail could be run more quickly and economically by riverboat. George requisitioned from Murray a small but swift steamer that he dubbed the *U.S. Mail* (1831).

With Peter Dohrman as its captain, the *Mail* did the Steubenville–Wheeling run for four years until another Murray craft, the *Postboy* (1835), replaced it, with M.E. Lucas as its captain. Lucas was later replaced by his engineer, John S. Devenny, who also captained the next Steubenville mail boat, the *Wabash* (1838). Other boats followed, not listed in the standard sources, which suggests that they, too, may have been made by Murray: the *Cabinet* (1843–circa 1850), the *Viroqua* (early 1850s) and the *Convoy* (late 1850s).

With the rise of the steam locomotive at the start of the Civil War—and the strategic importance of the railway to that war—ship production on

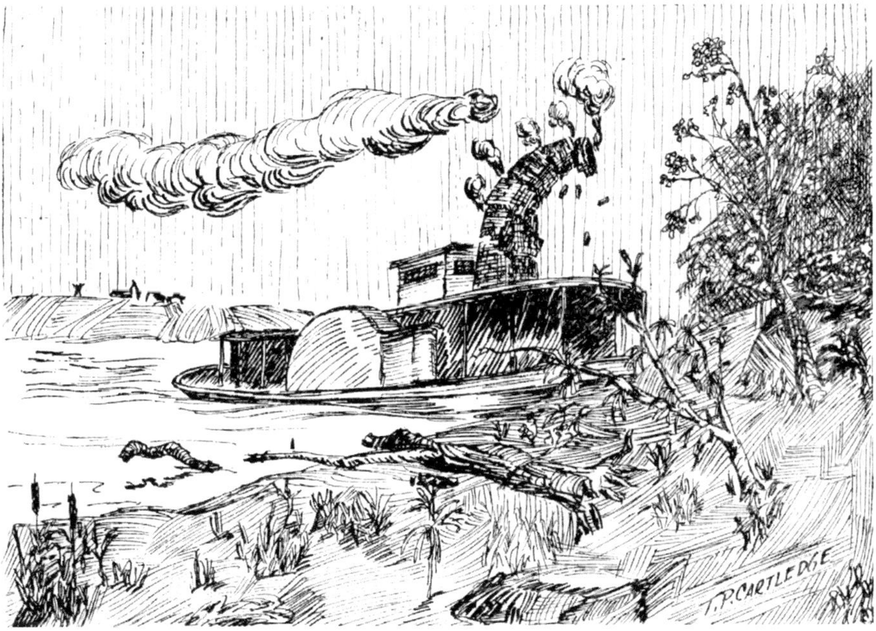

The brick smokestack of Steubenville's first steamboat, the *Bezaleel Wells* (1819), did not survive its maiden voyage. *Steubenville Sesquicentennial* Souvenir Book.

the Ohio began to decline. Yet Steubenville's steamers and their captains were not inactive in the war. Steubenville's shipyard commemorated the city's entry into the war by producing the patriotically named *Union* (1861), which serviced the Wheeling market. It was at the siege of Vicksburg, however, that Steubenville captain George O'Neal—son of the legendary Steubenville steamboat captain Abner O'Neal—showed his mettle. After Sherman had taken Hayne's Bluff on May 19, 1863, Union steamers controlled the Mississippi. But before that—when O'Neal piloted a Union gunboat—Confederate artillery on those heights could pick off the Union boats at will. O'Neal was one of those pilots who ran full speed into a hail of cannonballs to give naval gun support for Sherman's advance. The prospect of death on the water would traumatize O'Neal again in peacetime twenty years later, but that story is for the next chapter.

PART III

River and Rail: Early Transportation in Steubenville

Flatboats and Keelboats

Long before the steam era, Steubenville's fortunes were tied to the river. However, the "natural" river—the river before such improvements as damming and dredging removed navigational hazards—made shipping difficult. For one thing, river water had an inconvenient habit of flowing only one way. Barges and flatboats could carry several tons of goods, but they only floated downstream. Once cargo reached New Orleans, the barges were sold for lumber, and the pilots would buy horses and ride back to start the process again.

Keelboats were a different story, though. They could travel in both directions, though of course upstream was harder and slower. Teams of men poled the keelboats slowly upstream or pulled them with cables from the shore. Sometimes they would also use sail power. A return trip from New Orleans to Steubenville could take a month or more.

Snags and sandbars were not the only dangers to Ohio Valley boatmen, however. Many backwoods opportunists knew that the flatboats and keelboats held thousands of dollars' worth of merchandise and that the boatmen bled as easy as anyone. Boatmen knew that they were taking their lives into their hands with each trip and that even if they could avoid robbery, an accident could easily sink their entire inventory. What, then, could possibly make such a trip worthwhile? That was simple: the enormous profit.

Steubenville's earliest merchants—Hans Wilson and John England, for example—depended on receiving trade goods by keelboat. A merchant who commandeered his own flatboats was a wholesaler, though, and the biggest in Steubenville was Martin Andrews. Andrews had made his first fortune in furs—buying cheap from the trappers in the valley and carting them in six-horse Conestoga wagons over the mountains to Philadelphia, where they brought considerable profit. Buying flatboats with his profit, Andrews filled them with Ohio Valley products—tons of flour from several mills on the Ohio and its tributaries and salt from shallow mines and natural licks, as well as salted meat bought from local hunters. Andrews invested in all three commodities and accompanied the shipments to New Orleans so that he could bring back the cash himself. Some of the profit, however, he brought back in coffee, which he supplied to Steubenville stores. On one trip, he was jostled and relieved of his entire net of $1,700—in an era when good farmland was selling for $1 per acre and a good house might go for $500.

It might be supposed that the advent of steam power to push against the current brought the end of the one-way flatboats. Far from it. By 1845, after a quarter-century of Steubenville steamboating, there were 1,200 steamships on the Ohio and Mississippi, but there were more than 4,000 flatboats. Steamboats could carry considerably more, but even so, the flatboats accounted for fully a third of the annual tonnage shipped downriver in the mid-nineteenth century.

The modern Ohio Valley resident assumes that the locks and dams put into place in the early twentieth century were the first man-made controls of the navigable depth of the Ohio. This is not so. Even before the steamboat era, navigators dredged sandbars, removed snags and built cutoff dams in back channels and wing dikes in main channels to maximize depth for navigation. On May 24, 1824, President James Monroe signed the first Inland Waterways Improvement Act to fund this work, and the Army Corps of Engineers was put to it. In the Steubenville area, the biggest navigation problem in the early 1800s was Brown's Island, which diverted the Ohio into two shallow channels. In 1836, dredging and damming deepened both channels sufficiently to allow the heaviest-laden ships to pass through.

The narrowness of the channels, however, meant that only one boat at a time could pass on either side of an island like Brown's Island just upriver from Steubenville or Mingo Island just downriver. When steamboats became the norm, with deep, steam-powered whistles, a signaling system was devised. Not following the signals would lead to the greatest river disaster in Steubenville history. And that brings us back to George O'Neal.

Disaster on the River

It was a warm Fourth of July in 1882. Although it was a holiday for most of Steubenville, George O'Neal was on duty. Like his father before him, George was Steubenville's wharf master. When old Abner O'Neal died in 1878, the city couldn't imagine its waterfront without an O'Neal in charge. So George was appointed to the task, and tonight he faced his fourth Independence Day in the boathouse at the foot of Market Street.

To get a sense of what George was up against this holiday night, let's think of him like the state trooper who pulls patrol duty New Year's Eve. Yes, people just want to have a good time, but it's your job to keep the highways safe. Well, that was George's dilemma. In his charge was the biggest highway in these parts: the Ohio River. And tonight it would be teeming with pleasure craft, filled (perhaps overfilled) with people untrained in river safety, and the shores would be thick with boys armed with explosives, hoping to get a rise out of the passing steamboat parties with sudden colorful explosions of rockets and Roman candles.

Thad Thomas, a level-headed captain of George's generation, had stopped at the Steubenville wharf that morning to pick up passengers in his excursion boat *Scioto*. George and Thad had known each other for many years, working together on the run to Wheeling. They had met for lunch virtually every day in Wheeling for several years, when George ran the *Abner O'Neal* daily from Steubenville to Wheeling and Thad ran the *Telegram* from Clarington to Wheeling. Now it was a pleasure cruise, and Thad had his two sons with him—Clint, who was apprenticed to the pilot and was learning his father's trade, and little Dan.

The *Scioto*'s excursion was just beginning—it had come down from Wellsburg—but already the craft looked full. The *Scioto* was built seven years ago as a mail carrier but was refitted earlier this year as a pleasure steamer. It had a ballroom put in—the popular Milholland Brass Band of Wellsburg could be heard winding down as Captain Thomas took on Steubenville passengers—and there was a banquet room and a piano lounge below.

Though it was O'Neal's official duty to warn his friend against overcrowding, he knew that Thomas's employers, the Wheeling and Parkersburg Transportation Company, also employed a bank of lawyers who made life hard for local petty officials who gave them trouble, so Thomas probably received no more than a friendly warning when the *Scioto* took off for Moundsville.

That had been this morning. Now dusk was gathering, and O'Neal was herding the last of the Steubenville excursionists for the night. Captain Inglebright was on his way downriver with a more sober group in the *John Lomas*. With the growing darkness, though, the fireworks would be out soon.

DIRECTORY OF STEUBENVILLE.

W. & W. M. O'NEAL,

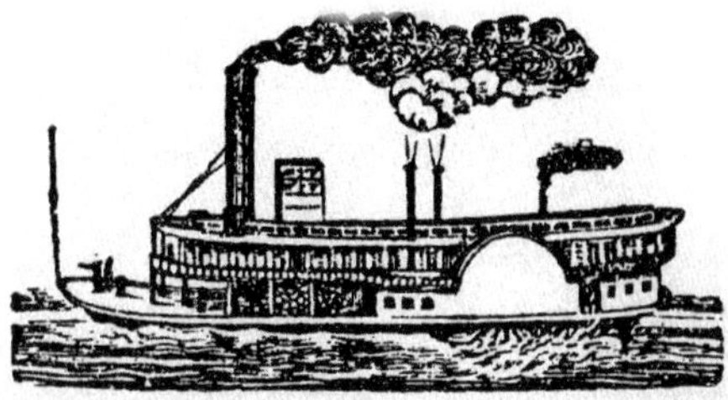

FORWARDING & COMMISSION MERCHANTS.

Ware House near Corner of Washington and Water Streets,
Wharf Boat at Market Street Landing,

STEUBENVILLE, O.

STEAM BOATS SUPPLIED WITH PROVISIONS AT ALL TIMES.

The O'Neals were Steubenville's foremost family in the riverboat trade. Whitacre and William ran this packet service. *1850 Directory, Ohio Collection, Schiappa Library.*

Firecrackers, however, would prove the least of Captain O'Neal's problems. Just as the darkness started to deepen, about an hour after the *Lomas* had left—it was nearing 9:30 p.m.—Charlie Staples ran into the wharf master's office. About ten years prior, Staples had taken over the sawmill that had replaced Murray's boatyard. He was determined to make it a shipyard again and had even built a fine steamer for the American centennial a few years ago, which he named, aptly enough, the *'76*.

Staples wasn't here to talk business, though. He had news: an accident just below Mingo. Hundreds in the water. No one knows how many dead, but they're pulling out the bodies.

George O'Neal fired up the steamboat that bore his father's name. The *Abner* had not made a run that day, so it would take some time to build up steam. Meanwhile he sent one of the office boys to the Western Union office—only a block away, on the corner of Water and Market. O'Neal knew that any details about the accident would come there first: reporters and police would be telegraphing details, and whatever could be heard there would be more reliable than the rumors in the shipyard.

The news from the telegraph office was chilling. Just below Mingo, the *Lomas*, which had just left Steubenville, had struck the heavy-laden *Scioto* broadside at full speed, tearing a hole below the waterline and forward, near

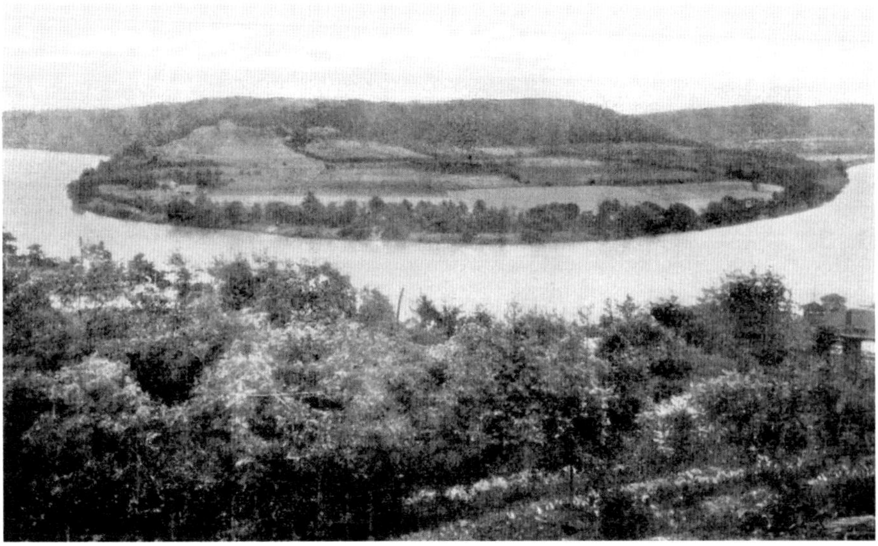

Half Moon Farm, just upriver from Steubenville. *Ohio Collection, Schiappa Library.*

the coal box, sending fire shooting over the deck. The fire was not the worst of it, however. The majority of the passengers were below deck when the collision occurred.

As the *Abner* approached Mingo Island, the clouds had cleared a little. It was just after ten o'clock, and the full moon showed more than any river veteran would want to see. Only about half of the *Scioto*'s cabin, the highest point of the vessel, was visible above the waterline. Skiffs still crisscrossed the scene, grimly trolling for bodies, but they made way for the *Abner O'Neal.* Through the glass below the hurricane deck, the wharf master could see the piano, upside down in two feet of water. Shards of glass and furniture were strewn about and life jackets floated uselessly.

The *Lomas* was still docked at Mingo Junction when the *Abner* arrived. George found a berth for the *Abner* and boarded the other boat. There was Inglebright, guiding the people onto the shore. They were oddly silent for such a big crowd; some were still dripping river water. Inglebright said that he had been going back and forth to pick up survivors ever since the crash. It was the little skiffs from Mingo that had the harder task of bringing in the lifeless bodies.

The last news from the Western Union office before O'Neal left Steubenville was that all of the reporters were chartering a special train to take them down to the crash sight. In addition to his primary duty to rescue survivors, George must have wanted to find Thomas before those jackals of the press hounded him and his two boys.

Such a characterization of the paparazzi may seem too modern, but the journalistic tradition of the "live" report from the scene did not begin in the twenty-first century. The first electronic, speed-of-light communication was not radio but rather the telegraph. The Ohio Valley newspaper accounts of the *Scioto* disaster read like transcripts of CNN coverage of a similar crisis. On-the-spot eyewitness reports were wired immediately to the home office, and the papers printed them verbatim in present tense under a timeline:

> *MINGO JUNCTION—HALF PAST 12. It is a bright moonlight night, and this accounts for the fact, as it now appears, that the loss is so small as compared with first reports. The latest word is that the number will probably not exceed ten. Will dispatch further as soon as additional particulars can be ascertained.*
>
> *MOUTH OF SHORT CREEK—1:30 A.M. I have just seen Arthur McNally, who lives at Short Creek and who was an eye witness of the whole scene, standing at his front door immediately opposite where the collision occurred.*

O'Neal found Thomas amid the chaos and ushered the distraught captain to a stateroom on the *Abner O'Neal*. Thomas was tearing his hair, weeping alternately over the loss of his career and the fate of his boy. Clint had been found, helping the *Lomas* crew evacuate the *Scioto*, but little Dan was still missing. Captain O'Neal helped the sobbing Thomas into the room and stood guard at the door. George O'Neal was not as big a man as his father, but he had made a career of getting the most muscular men in the valley to do as he ordered. He could handle the press.

The reporters arrived on the Virginia side—even twenty years after the separation of the new state from Virginia, locals, especially in the river trade, still omitted the "West" from West Virginia—on the Pittsburgh, Wheeling and Kentucky rail line. Captain O'Neal stood his ground and insisted that only friends and family would be allowed to see Captain Thomas. But when George opened the door to let in an old friend, a Wheeling *Intelligencer* reporter was able to hear (or perhaps reconstruct) the frantic cries that came out over the transom:

> *Oh, my God; my God, John, it was awful. I can see the poor wretches down in the water, and Dan—oh, where is my boy? We were going along so nicely and in two or three hours more would have been all right and the care would have been off my mind. I was in the cabin, boys, seeing that everything was kept straight, when I heard the whistle blowing. I knew*

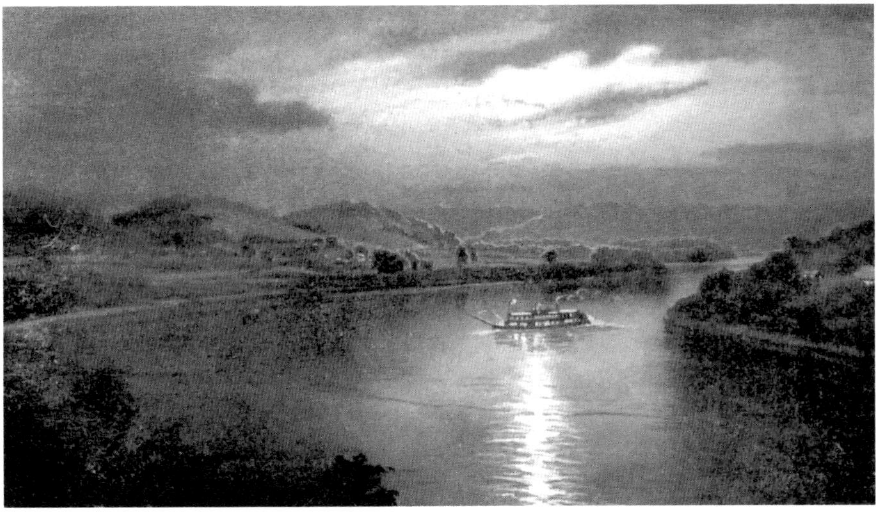

Steubenville river scene from a postcard. *Ohio Collection, Schiappa Library.*

> *something was wrong, and, going out on the guards, I climbed up the jack-post to the hurricane deck and yelled to Dave to back her. He answered that that was what he was doing but it was too late and the crash came.*

"Dave" was David Keller, the pilot who had been at the wheel of the *Scioto* with Thomas's son, Clint. He had been taken immediately after the crash down to Wheeling to report to the owners of the *Scioto* (and their lawyers). They appeared just before dawn, about 5:30 a.m., on the company's flagship, the *Welcome*, with Dave himself at the wheel. Behind them, O'Neal saw the familiar outline of the *Telegram*, the packet Thomas had commanded in the daily Wheeling run from his hometown of Clarington, Ohio, fifty miles downriver. Just an hour earlier, Thomas had vowed that he would not leave the site until Dan was found. Shortly after, however, Dan's lifeless body was pulled from the Ohio. The body was lifted onto the *Telegram*. George O'Neal found the grieving father a berth on his old ship and sent father and son home.

The Steubenville and Indiana Railroad

The interplay of rail and river travel in the *Scioto* disaster of 1882 typified the transportation picture of the upper Ohio Valley in the second half of the nineteenth century. Though the Civil War halted boat production in

Steubenville—an anomaly at a time when most Northern river cities were rushing to supply gunboats and transports to the army—competition to move supplies downriver to the soldiers increased the river traffic near Steubenville.

The iron horse had already begun to challenge the steamboat in Steubenville, however. By mid-century, the population of Steubenville had tripled since the appearance of the *Bezaleel Wells*. In the 1820 U.S. Census, Steubenville was not separated from the Jefferson County population figures. The town had taken its own census, however, in 1817, showing 2,032 men, women and children in the city limits. In 1850, the U.S. Census showed 6,140. Steubenville's merchants saw no reason that such growth should not continue, and they argued that Steubenville needed its own railroad line.

James Means, who had been making iron and steel in Steubenville since 1830, began getting orders for rails and spikes in 1844 for the Cleveland and Pittsburgh line, which was projected to extend only as far south as Wellsburg. Means realized that a relatively small investment could secure a line from Steubenville to Wellsburg, linking them to the Cleveland road that was already being extended west to the Indiana border. And so, in 1847, Means and a dozen other Steubenville visionaries formed the Steubenville & Indiana (S&I) Railroad Company, issuing stock and securing rights-of-way. Steubenville city council authorized the purchase of $100,000 of the stock in the name of the city; the Township of Steubenville bought another $100,000, and private citizens a third—which means that, along with $30,000 from Cross Creek Township, the entire operation was capitalized by Steubenville itself.

Some of the charter members dropped out, but others became so invested in the future of the railroad that they abandoned everything else. James Parks, who had not been one of the original baker's dozen but joined the board in 1850, sold his dry goods store on Fourth and Market to devote all his time (and capital) to railroad business. Another major investor, Daniel Kilgore of Cadiz, not only gave up his business but also his home in Cadiz, moving to Steubenville to concentrate on fundraising in the city. The newspapers, in fact, seemed to credit the success of the Steubenville and Indiana to Kilgore's personal magnetism and drive (the adjectives in the Pittsburgh *Patriot* were "pushing"—intended as a compliment—and "go-ahead").

It was all the more tragic, then, that Daniel Kilgore did not live to see the Steubenville & Indiana become a reality. In mid-July 1851, Kilgore traveled to Pittsburgh to supervise the engraving of $1,000 bonds for the company. On July 20, he left Pittsburgh (by rail) for New York to put the bonds on the market. In New York, that most competitive of markets, the bonds sold

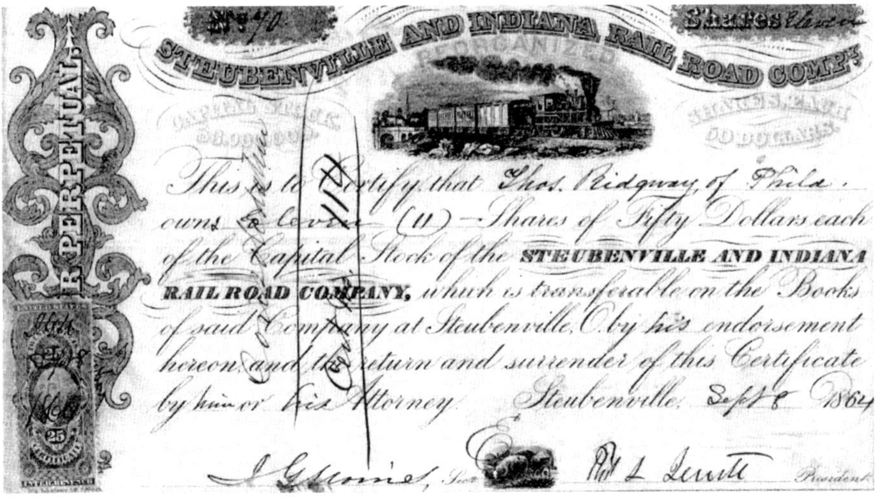

Stock certificate, Steubenville & Indiana Railroad, 1864. Later that year, the S&I was absorbed by the Pittsburgh, Columbus & Cincinnati. *Ohio Collection, Schiappa Library.*

instantly—again the papers credited Kilgore's charm. "We cannot for a moment doubt his success," proclaimed the Steubenville *Herald*, "for he is never unsuccessful in any enterprise he undertakes." The sale of the bonds proved to be Kilgore's last success. On December 12, 1851, two years and ten days before the first locomotive pulled into Steubenville, Kilgore died peacefully in his home in Steubenville at the age of fifty-seven.

On March 10, 1853, Steubenville City Council officially approved the right-of-way for the Steubenville & Indiana (jointly with the Cleveland and Pittsburgh line). On May 26, 1853, the first locomotive arrived by flatboat; a month later, on June 29, two more were unloaded. The engines were built by the Rogers, Ketchum and Grosvenor works in Patterson, New Jersey. Not a single engine from that year remains, though the famous General of 1855, the Confederate locomotive nearly stolen by Yankee spies in the Civil War, would be close to what the Steubenville looked like: a wide smokestack to accommodate wood burning (though the Wells and its fellows burned coal), with a four-four-zero configuration (four lead wheels, four driving wheels and no trailing wheels). The General can still be seen at the Southern Museum of Civil War and Locomotive History in Kennesaw, Georgia.

The Steubenville & Indiana Company named its first engine the Bezaleel Wells and engines two and three the James Ross and the Steubenville, respectively. On August 23, the first two passenger cars were received (one first class and one second class), though the track for the line was not yet

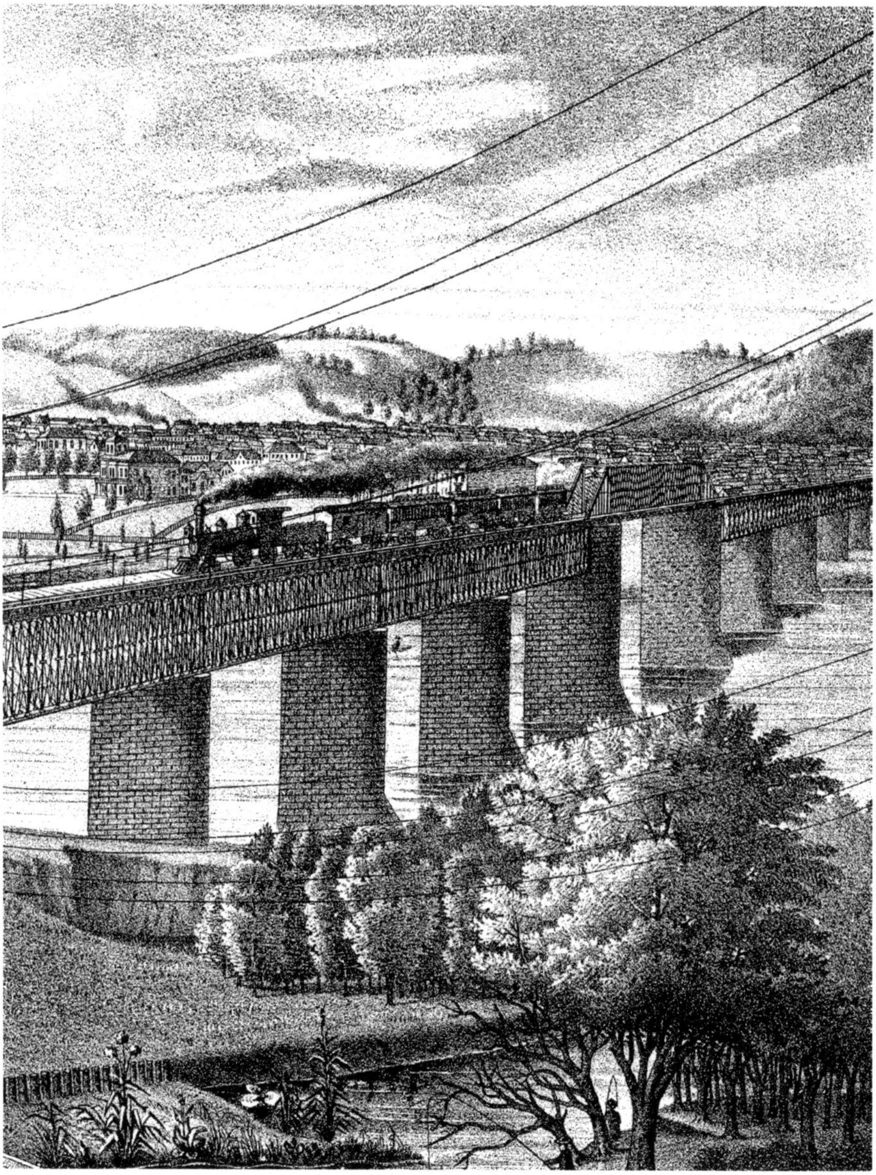

Panhandle Bridge of the Pittsburgh, Columbus & Cincinnati Railroad, Steubenville, completed in 1868. *Caldwell's* History of Belmont and Jefferson Counties.

completed. Finally, on December 22, 1853, as Steubenville's early Christmas present, the Bezaleel Wells chuffed across Market Street, offering free rides to all comers and opening the railroad era in Steubenville.

In the first two months of operation, the Steubenville & Indiana sold 6,734 passenger tickets for a total revenue of $2,013.10, with only $892.97 in operating expenses. The line went from Steubenville to Unionport, with stops at Mingo, Goulds, West End, Smithfield, Reed's Mills, Bloomfield and the terminus, Union Port, where passengers could change trains for other destinations. Fares for the full run to Union Port were $0.60; minimum fare for shorter distances, $0.10.

Most histories of Steubenville mention only the three locomotives named above. But within a few weeks of opening, the Steubenville & Indiana actually had eight working engines and 174 cars. The remaining five engines were named the Newark, the Coshocton, the Fairy, the Glide and, to honor the late president of the S&I, the Daniel Kilgore.

Like most small railroad companies, the Steubenville & Indiana did not last long as an independent venture. In 1864, the S&I was absorbed into the Pittsburgh, Columbus & Cincinnati, popularly known as the Panhandle Line (though, in fact, the S&I had been in receivership since 1859 due to disputes with shareholders). When the PC&C was in turn bought up, the parent company, the Pennsylvania Railroad, kept the local name by calling it the "Panhandle Division of the Pennsylvania."

Although Steubenville's own railroad did not last long, the city became a footnote in railroad history one more time in 1869. It was here that George Westinghouse Jr. tested his invention, the Westinghouse air brake. Steubenville was close enough to Westinghouse's Pittsburgh base to be convenient but was on a line that could be bypassed in case of an accident. The Steubenville test proved that air pumped from a reservoir could stop a heavy locomotive, though the chain reaction of the cars behind it bumping into the engine indicated that more work would be needed. Based on his experience in Steubenville, Westinghouse would later redesign the air brake with separate air reservoirs in each car.

The Wells, the Kilgore, the Steubenville and all the rest of the Steubenville engines were retired after less than two decades of service. A humorist wrote a wistful piece that appeared in the Steubenville *Weekly Gazette* on April 22, 1881, lamenting the fate of the Steubenville, which had been sold to the railroad car shops in Dennison, Ohio (where the 1873 Dennison Depot still houses a rail museum), to power a sawmill. The writer gave a brief biography of the engine in its own voice:

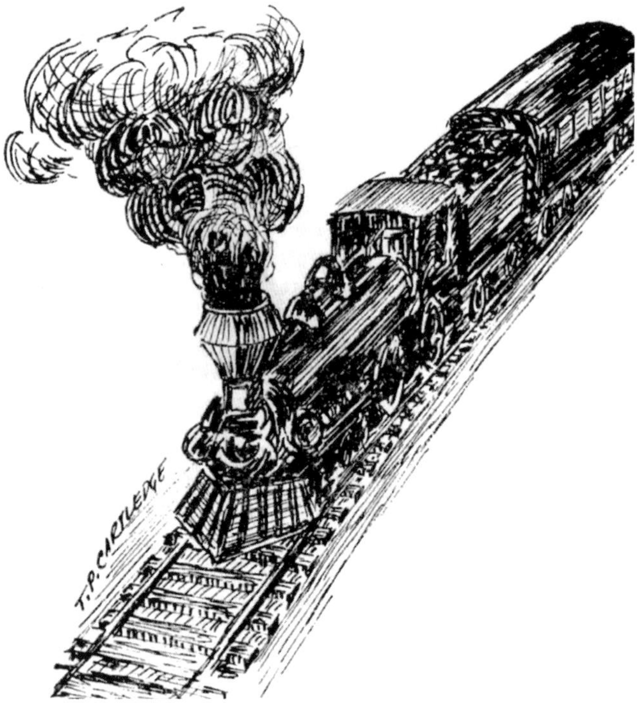

Though no specimens survive of the 1853 Rogers locomotives made for Steubenville, this 1947 sketch is probably accurate. *Steubenville Sesquicentennial* Souvenir Book.

Why sir, I have pulled the President of the United States; I have carried General Grant when he was only a captain in the army, after he came back from Mexico; I have had five United States Senators and the Governor of Ohio riding behind me at one time; I've run down the road on the Fourth of July, brasses brighter than the sunlight, cab and tender and stack just a flutter with flags, Washington's picture on the headlight and every station just cheering like mad when I came thundering in; I've fought snow drifts that swirled like breakers as high as the dome; I've dashed over bridges that fairly swayed and trembled with the flood that chafed and foamed at pier and tugged at piling and trestlework; in the day and the sunshine, in the night and the storm I've seen this road. I've made my running time between stations right along, I never killed a man that humored my temper and handled me right; I'm the oldest live engine on the "Panhandle," and here I am to-day, sawing wood like a horse power.

Although passenger rail service has all but vanished from American consciousness—and the Panhandle along with it—one last vestige of Steubenville's own rail service hung on until the end of the twentieth century: the tracks themselves. In 1991, Conrail purchased the Panhandle line from

Mingo to Columbus from Ohio Central Railroad. The announcement was made at a press conference in the capital by Ohio governor Mike DeWine, but scarcely anyone in Steubenville noticed.

Whiskey, Mail and the Overland Stage

Given the story that the building of Fort Steuben was motivated by whiskey, it might not surprise the Steubenville historian to discover that Ohio Valley stills may have provided the primary drive to build Steubenville's early roads and stagecoach lines. Michael Roberts, an enterprising metalsmith, supplied most of the farmers in the upper Ohio Valley with distilling equipment in the first two decades of the town's existence.

The predominance of stills in Jefferson County circa 1820 was not just a function of thirst or the call of demon rum. It was also a function of the prohibitive cost of shipping raw corn and grain as opposed to distilling its essence into something more potable and portable. Much, if not most, of the produce of these stills was shipped down the river—and some via the more arduous overland route to Philadelphia and other eastern cities. And that required roads.

The trip over the Alleghenies was usually made by six-horse Conestogas over little more than Indian trails. Local deliveries—such as Roberts's distillation equipment—required improved roads from Steubenville to all the outlying towns. Because Roberts was the first to look into the problem of adequate roads, he naturally developed the first stage lines, and because he developed the first stage lines, Roberts became the first mail carrier in Steubenville.

As an engineer (no one who manufactures stills can be thought of under a lesser title), Roberts understood the new process of macadamization. Today that word is associated with tar-and-gravel roads, but early macadamized roads did not use tar to bind the gravel. Instead, roads were dug out as channels and then layered with rock of increasing fineness until the top layer could be packed down with horse drawn iron rollers. The result was a gravel road that was so tightly packed that it would seem more like pavement and would not wash out easily.

With these roads and a stable of fast horses, Roberts began sending stages from Steubenville in 1816, at first every few days. By 1829, though, under Roberts's successor, George A. Dohrman, six stages left Steubenville daily, each in different directions. Fares were five cents per mile, and the usual pace was just under eight miles per hour. Horses were exchanged usually about every twelve miles (that's why they were called "stage" coaches—they traveled in stages), and the inns at which the horses were changed thrived by offering every comfort to the traveler. For the next twenty years, until the advent of the Steubenville & Indiana Railroad, the stagecoach was the fastest and most comfortable way to travel in and out of Steubenville.

PART IV

EDUCATION

THE STEUBENVILLE FEMALE SEMINARY

Very few nineteenth-century institutions still register on the twenty-first-century consciousness in Steubenville. One that does is the Steubenville Female Seminary. The buildings and grounds have long disappeared, and the school closed its doors over a century ago, in 1898. However, the image of Mother Beatty, the founder and guiding spirit, has become Steubenville legend. Of all the people in Steubenville's history I would most like to have met, Hetty Elizabeth Beatty surely tops the list.

It may be that her husband, Dr. Charles Clinton Beatty, had all the credentials: a doctorate from Princeton, ordination (and later a national office) in the Presbyterian Church and a Steubenville connection that went back to the days of the fort—but we already told that part of the story under "The Fort." So, sure, Reverend C.C. Beatty had the goods to run a girls' school, but he wasn't a girl. Neither was Hetty anymore, but she had been one once, and she knew what girls needed in a school.

Just as important, Hetty knew what Reverend Beatty needed. Just before his arrival in Steubenville, Beatty's first wife, Lydia, had died in childbirth. Hetty Davis—that was her name then—felt sorry for the young widower. No Presbyterian minister could be truly successful, she reasoned, without a good wife. If she was scrupulous in consoling the newly widowed minister, and if she spent a good deal of time with him making plans for a girls' school—well, even ministers are human. Could she help it if he fell in love with her? They were married in 1827.

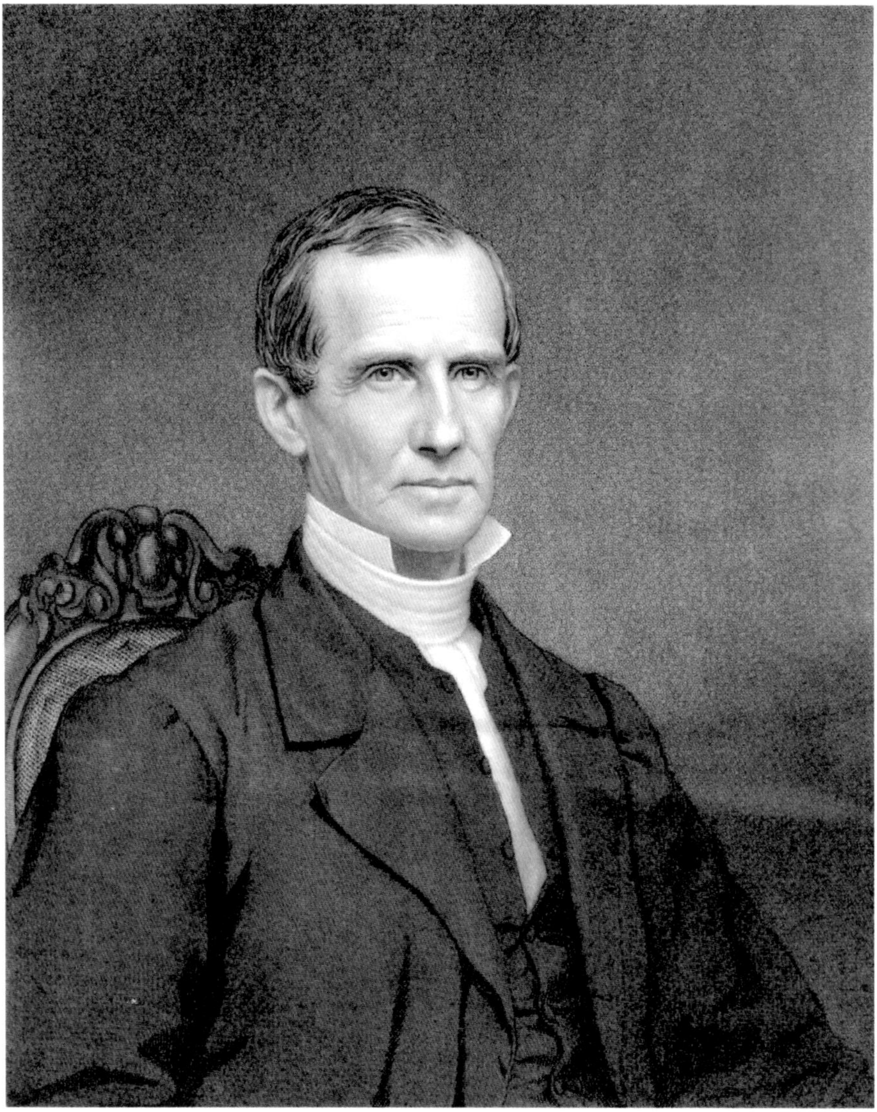

Charles C. Beatty of the Steubenville Female Seminary. Engraved in 1862. *Ohio Collection, Schiappa Library.*

The following spring, Mr. and Mrs. Beatty took an extensive tour of the East, especially New England, inspecting the most prestigious academies for girls in the nation. They took the best practices they saw, informed by Hetty's own education in Louisville, Kentucky, and brought their notes back to Steubenville. In December 1828, Dr. Beatty bought an empty lot on High

Street, below Adams, offering access to the river. By 1828, packets arrived every day in Steubenville from up and down the Ohio and Mississippi, so Beatty constructed a landing before he even put up the school building. Advertising heavily throughout the nation, Mr. and Mrs. Beatty within a year were able to open their doors to about a dozen pupils.

Opening day was April 13, 1829. Why April? Well, in the early nineteenth century, even urban America still functioned as an agricultural society. Coeducational and boys' schools met from October to March so that sons would be available for the heavy work seasons on the farm, planting and harvesting. The assumption was that daughters could be spared from that sort of work (though haymaking and grain harvest were often mixed-gender activities), so girls' schools typically met from April to September. The Steubenville Female Seminary followed this pattern for its first few years but switched to a September–March academic calendar before the first graduating class. By the 1880s, exams and commencement were in June.

The curriculum was rigorous, including all the touches of refinement expected of young ladies in the nineteenth century, such as painting, music and French, but it also included subjects that had been thought of as exclusively male territory, such as Latin, gymnastics, chemistry, trigonometry and astronomy. In the first year, only "Primary Class" students were accepted (ages twelve and thirteen); they were instructed in reading, spelling, writing, geography, natural history (what today we would call physical science), U.S. history (all fifty-three years of it!), grammar and arithmetic—all for a tuition of five dollars for the year.

The second year, 1830, brought in a new Primary Class, and the first pupils returned for the "Middle Class." Second-year girls, thirteen to fourteen years old, learned psychology, physiology, history, Biblical antiquities and more grammar and arithmetic in their first semester and natural philosophy, geography, Biblical antiquities, parsing (what would later become sentence diagramming) and algebra in their second. Their tuition was higher: six dollars per year.

The third year was the first to straddle calendar years, September 1831 to March 1832. For the first session, junior-year girls (fourteen and fifteen) took geometry, botany, history, algebra and geology; second session included geometry, trigonometry, chemistry, astronomy and theology, all for seven dollars per year.

Finally, the 1832–33 school year was the first to see a commencement. After bringing the senior girls through rhetoric, philosophy, political science, history and theology in first semester and literary criticism, moral philosophy, English literature, theology and an extensive review of the

TWENTY-NINTH ANNUAL

CATALOGUE AND OUTLINE

OF THE

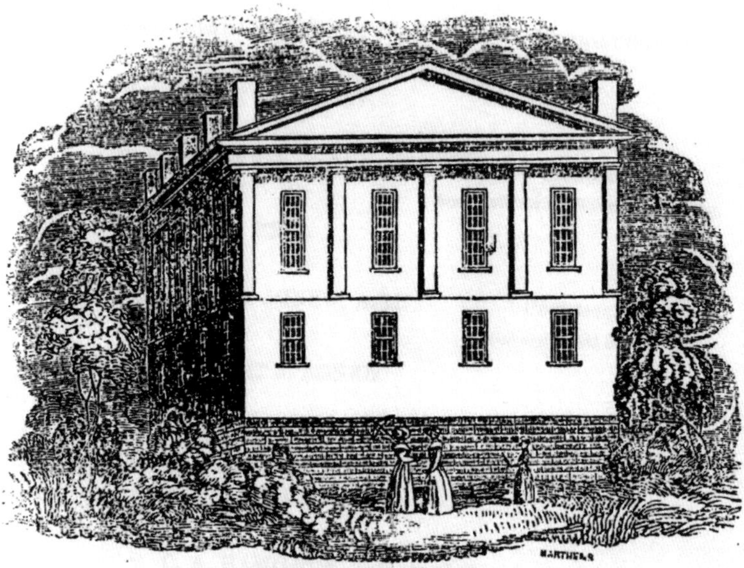

SEMINARY HALL.

FEMALE SEMINARY,

STEUBENVILLE, O.

FOR THE YEAR ENDING IN MARCH,

1858.

PRINTED BY W. S. HAVEN, CORNER OF MARKET AND SECOND STREETS, PITTSBURGH.

Catalogue of the Steubenville Female Seminary, 1858. *Ohio Collection, Schiappa Library.*

whole four years in the second semester, the Steubenville Female Seminary graduated a grand total of three young scholars in 1833. But those young women *were* scholars.

Readers wishing to duplicate the seminary's celebrated curriculum today could probably make a pretty fair approximation, because the later catalogues (1850s) included a list of the textbooks used. For history, sophomores read Royal Robbins's *Outlines of Ancient and Modern History on a New Plan* (1851). At a school reunion in 1873, Miss Nancy Sherrard (class of 1851), who had returned to the seminary as a teacher, offered a delightful parody of Robbins in giving a history of the school, then more than forty years old. "To those who have studied Robbins," she told alumnae and guests, "the division into periods will suggest itself, the principle events in each period, and the distinguished characters. At the close, after the manner of Robbins, we can give descriptions of dress, manners and customs, with the miscellaneous information, which is sometimes the most interesting part of the history."

Psychology, in the same session, used Isaac Watts's *The Improvement of the Mind* (1741), which modern educators would classify as logic rather than psychology. Parsing followed S.W. Clark's *A Practical Grammar* (1847). Even the hardiest of today's traditionalists might balk at Clark's arcane and complex method of sentence diagrams, which would not be replaced by the more familiar Reed-Kellogg system until 1877. But Mrs. Beatty's thirteen- and fourteen-year-old girls mastered it.

The junior-year theology text, Archibald Alexander's *Evidences of the Authenticity, Inspirations, and Canonical Authenticity of the Holy Scriptures* (1836), was pretty heavy going even for divinity students, but it was hardly a surprising choice. Dr. Alexander had been Beatty's mentor at Princeton. Adopting "Alexander's Evidences" guaranteed the sale of multiple copies of his old prof's book. Seniors in theology tackled Joseph Butler's *Analogy of Religion, Natural and Revealed* (1736), and for literary criticism it was Henry Home's (Lord Kames) *Elements of Criticism* (1762).

Our view of nineteenth-century education might be prejudiced by images of suffering in novels like *Jane Eyre* or *Tom Sawyer*, but the Female Seminary seems to have been remarkably like the best of modern schools in many ways. Discipline, for example. We have the image of the birch stick, but here is what Dr. Beatty's original brochure said about discipline:

> *Punishments are few, and reluctantly administered. All attempts at improvement are noticed and encouraged. The language of reproof is softened by the tones of affection, and does not penetrate the heart less deeply, nor influence the conduct less surely. It is wished and sought to*

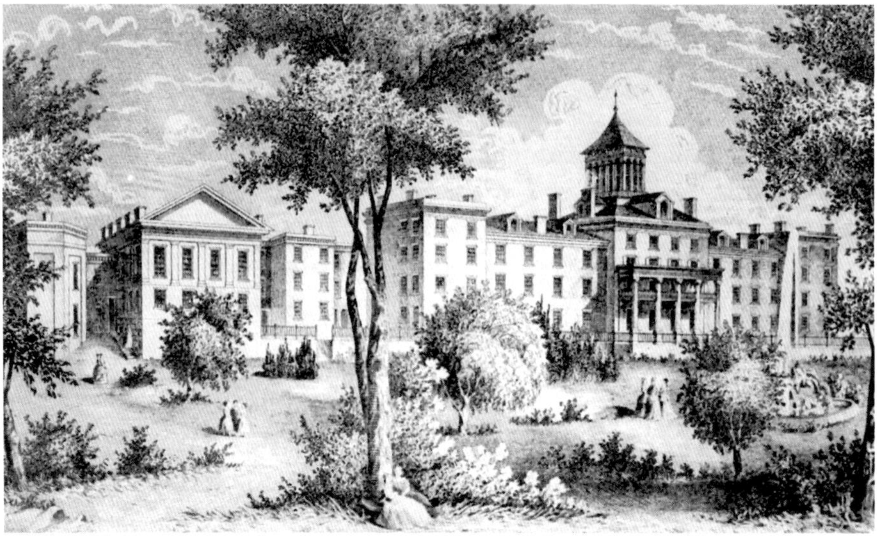

The Steubenville Female Seminary educated young women from 1829 to 1898. The block around this grove was protected by a large brick wall. *Ohio Collection, Schiappa Library.*

> *have all act from a sense of duty, and consider their own advancement, the approval of their consciences, the esteem of their teachers, the affection of their parents and friends, but above all, the approbation of an* ALL-SEEING GOD, *as the best rewards for correct deportment and studious improvement of time.*

And what about the moralism? Weren't schools back then oppressively moralistic? Huck Finn certainly thought so. To be sure, the Female Seminary was a religious school, run by a Presbyterian minister and his wife. To be sure, Reverend Beatty was the most vehement temperance leader in Steubenville for several decades. But both in Hetty Beatty's century and our own, there is a false tendency to assume that moral rectitude means not having any fun. Mother Beatty seems to have been the perfect antidote for that impression.

MOTHER BEATTY

Decades after they left the Steubenville Female Seminary, the graduates remembered the boisterous holidays there. Since many students came from other parts of the United States, very few could go home for Christmas in the pre-railroad days. One girl's New Year's letter home included the following description of Christmas at the seminary: "There was a plenty of noise, you know. There always is on such occasions. After prayers, there was such a crying of 'Merry Christmas!' for Christmas gifts that Mr. Beatty had to silence us." One assumes that the language of Mr. Beatty's reproof, however, was "softened by the tones of affection," as his brochure promised.

We expect a little high spirits on Christmas. Curiously, though, one of the most raucous holidays at the Female Seminary was Halloween. Halloween doubtless had a high profile in the early days of Steubenville. The earliest settlers of this region were predominantly Irish, and most of the American Halloween traditions were transplanted from Ireland. But the real reason for the seminary tradition of Halloween shenanigans may be the scenario recorded as an anecdote in the published biography of Mrs. Beatty. On one of those first Halloweens at the seminary, Mother Beatty stormed into the dormitory intent on quelling the giggling, thumping and yelling that accompany young girls letting loose, even in the 1830s.

According to the story, one particularly cool rabble-rouser greeted Mother Beatty's "What is the meaning of all this noise?" with studied nonchalance: "Why, Mother Beatty, we can't contain ourselves when we celebrate your birthday!" In fact, Hetty had been born October 31, 1802—a Halloween baby. A teacher of Hetty's caliber and experience certainly knew brittle excuses and apple-polishing flattery when she heard it. But maybe she also caught a glimpse of her earlier self in this teenage flimflam girl. After all, Mother Beatty must have had a little of that kind of moxie to start the first girls' school west of the Alleghenies. Maybe playing along was her way of holding on to the little girl in her. Whatever the reason, a rowdy Halloween romp, excused as a birthday fling for Mother Beatty, became an annual tradition.

Much of her life in the Female Seminary was a game for Hetty. One night she heard pebbles being tossed at the dormitory window, and she knew exactly what it must be: boys attempting secret late-night rendezvous with the girls under her charge. Now, this was in the day when all meetings between young men and women were to be chaperoned, but the way Mother Beatty handled the situation not only showed that she would indeed protect her girls, but also that she understood the natural psychology of boys.

She took off her cap and stuck her curly head out the window, knowing that in the dark her silhouette would look like that of a teenage girl. She pitched her voice accordingly and asked the boys their names. When they obliged, thinking they were talking to a sympathetic seminary girl, Mother Beatty resumed her normal voice and told them to leave.

Another instance of Mrs. Beatty's game playing was her literal game playing. Unlike some of the eastern girls' schools, the Steubenville Female

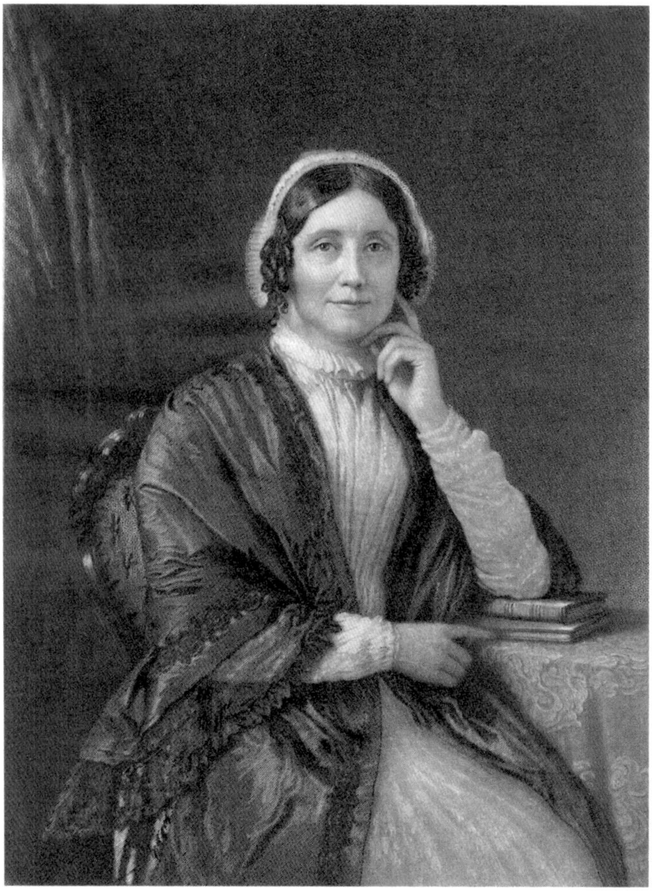

"Mother Beatty," Hetty Elizabeth Davis Beatty, was the driving force behind the Steubenville Female Seminary from 1829 until her death in 1876. *Ohio Collection, Schiappa Library.*

Seminary did not consider calisthenics exclusively for boys. Not only did Mother Beatty mandate organized sport for all her girls, but she also directed and participated in exercises herself. Granted, many of them were simple indoor running and chasing games. She threw herself into them, however. Particularly memorable to the ladies at the fortieth anniversary of the seminary was a game called "Who Wants to Buy a Big, Fat Hen?" The consensus was that, hands down, the best and liveliest imitation of a chicken, student or teacher, was Mother Beatty's.

The physical campus of the Steubenville Female Seminary grew throughout the years. In 1833, only two months after the graduation of the first class, Dr. Reid bought the lot immediately north of the school and two years later the lot to the south. As other lots became available, and as their profits from the school allowed, the Beattys bought up, one by one, in seven separate transactions, all of the adjoining lots. By 1841, the entire block was the seminary. Such autonomy gave a measure of security to the campus, allowing the school to put up a brick wall around the perimeter, 8 feet high, 600 feet along High Street and Water Street and 180 feet along Adams and South. Trees were planted and a fountain constructed, turning the quadrangle into a little oasis in the middle of a growing industrial city.

In 1856, the Reverend Dr. A.M. Reid was hired as principal, though Dr. Beatty retained nominal control and the title of superintendent. A decade later, Reid bought the entire school from the Beattys, who kept their residence in the seminary block and remained active participants in its exercises. On Halloween 1872, the school staged a lavish seventieth birthday celebration for Mother Beatty. The following year all of the four thousand or more graduates of the Steubenville Female Seminary (or those who were still alive) were invited to an all-class reunion. About seven hundred women arrived from all over the United States (particularly the Ohio and Mississippi Valleys).

Mother Beatty was still Mother Beatty at the reunion. When she rang the bell at dinner to call the ladies to order for the speakers, it was just like the old school days—too much like the old days, in fact. The dinner guests would not stop talking. Mother Beatty had to use the Mother Beatty shout one last time, and the Steubenville *Herald* was there to record it: "Young ladies, you must come to order! I cannot talk while you are talking!" The crowd burst into laughter, not just at the delight of hearing Mother Beatty sound like a principal again, but also at the irony of once again being called "young ladies," as many of them were now grandmothers. To the matriarch of the Female Seminary, though, they would always be young ladies.

The alumnae felt the same way. "We are all girls today," said Nancy Sharrard, now herself a teacher but twenty-two years earlier a student of Mrs. Beatty's. "We forget to-day the cares, the anxieties, and afflictions that have made some of us gray, and we are all again the bright, happy girls that we were when we looked out upon the great life of the world from within the walls of this Seminary."

There would be no celebration to equal that reunion in the remaining twenty-five years of the institution. The city held a celebration on the seminary grounds for the centennial of American independence on July 4, 1876, but Mrs. Hetty Beatty was too infirm to attend. The next day she died, at age seventy-four.

Dr. Charles Beatty died in 1882. Dr. Reid kept the institution going, but soon even he was too old to handle the day-to-day operations. He first turned them over to a new minister, but in 1888 he struck on the novel idea of having a Female Seminary with female administrators. It was at that

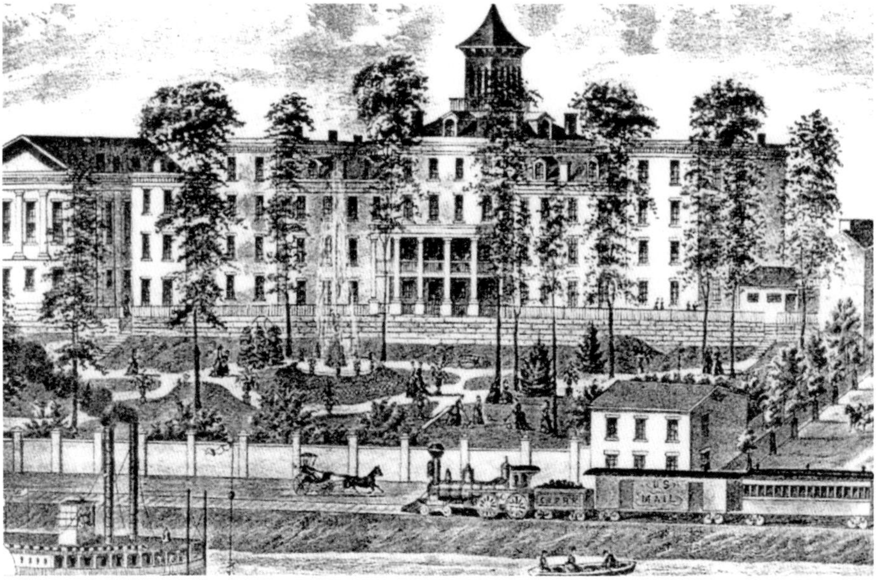

The Steubenville Female Seminary, seen from the river, 1870. The steamboat in the foreground was the *Arlington*, which served here from 1869 to 1873. *Ohio Collection, Schiappa Library*.

time that the seminary became the summer home of the Boston Musical Institute, offering local students tutelage under some of the finest European music scholars.

It did not prove enough to pay the bills, though. In 1898, the seminary closed for good. The pleasant grove became a lumber yard, and the brick wall was knocked down.

Buchanan's Academy

The Female Seminary was not, of course, the first (nor the last) great educational institution in Steubenville. As a pioneer settlement of the Northwest Territory, Steubenville was expected—mandated, in fact—to set aside a portion of its township for education. In 1805, Mr. Black opened a school in his home on Market Street just west of Fifth. But the first building put up expressly for schooling in Steubenville was, like so many of Steubenville's firsts, the work of Bezaleel Wells. In 1807, Wells donated a lot on High Street, built the "Little Red Schoolhouse" (as it became known long before that phrase was an American cliché) and installed James Thompson as the first town schoolmaster. The school was opened to boys and girls at a rate of $2.50 per term ($5.00 for the full school year). The same year, 1807, saw the publication of Noah Webster's *United States Speller*, which was used in the new schoolhouse along with Lindley Murray's *Introduction to the English Reader*.

The town's school simply taught the three Rs, but a few blocks away, on Market Street, the Reverend Dr. George Buchanan had loftier educational goals. In 1814, thirty-one-year-old Buchanan opened the first classical academy in the West. Buchanan had been among the first generation, indeed the first class, of theologians who did not have to go to Europe for their advanced degrees. Just as Buchanan had completed his MA at Dickinson College in 1804, the Union Theological Seminary opened its doors with the first doctor of divinity program in the United States. Buchanan entered on opening day and studied under one of the seminary's founders, John Mitchell Mason.

Upon completion of his degree (and ordination), the Reverend Dr. Buchanan established several reformed Presbyterian churches in the western frontier of Pennsylvania before receiving a call to take over a pulpit in Steubenville. There, in the basement of the rectory on Market Street, Dr. Buchanan began teaching a classical curriculum of logic, rhetoric and (Latin) grammar, preparing his students for college or university study. President Lincoln's secretary of war, Edwin M. Stanton, was one of Buchanan's students.

All three of Buchanan's sons studied in their father's school, and all went on to higher education. The two oldest, John and Joseph, were both ordained ministers, and Joseph also continued his father's other career as an educator, serving as superintendent of Jefferson County schools for two generations. The youngest, James, became a physician in Pittsburgh.

The most memorable story of Reverend George Buchanan in Steubenville, though, has nothing to do with education, but rather with his fighting spirit and his renowned horse, Punch. It was the waning days of the so-called War of 1812 (which lasted well into 1814). Reverend Buchanan had just moved to Steubenville with his young wife, Mary; none of their sons had been born yet. Though a man of God, Buchanan had the fire and bearing of a military man, and the men of the regiment then stationed in Steubenville chose him as their chaplain.

When report came, however, that a detachment of English soldiers and Indian warriors was making for Steubenville, the chaplain seemed to be the only one who wasn't afraid. Gathering the regiment into the courthouse, Reverend Buchanan laid aside the gospel text about turning the other cheek

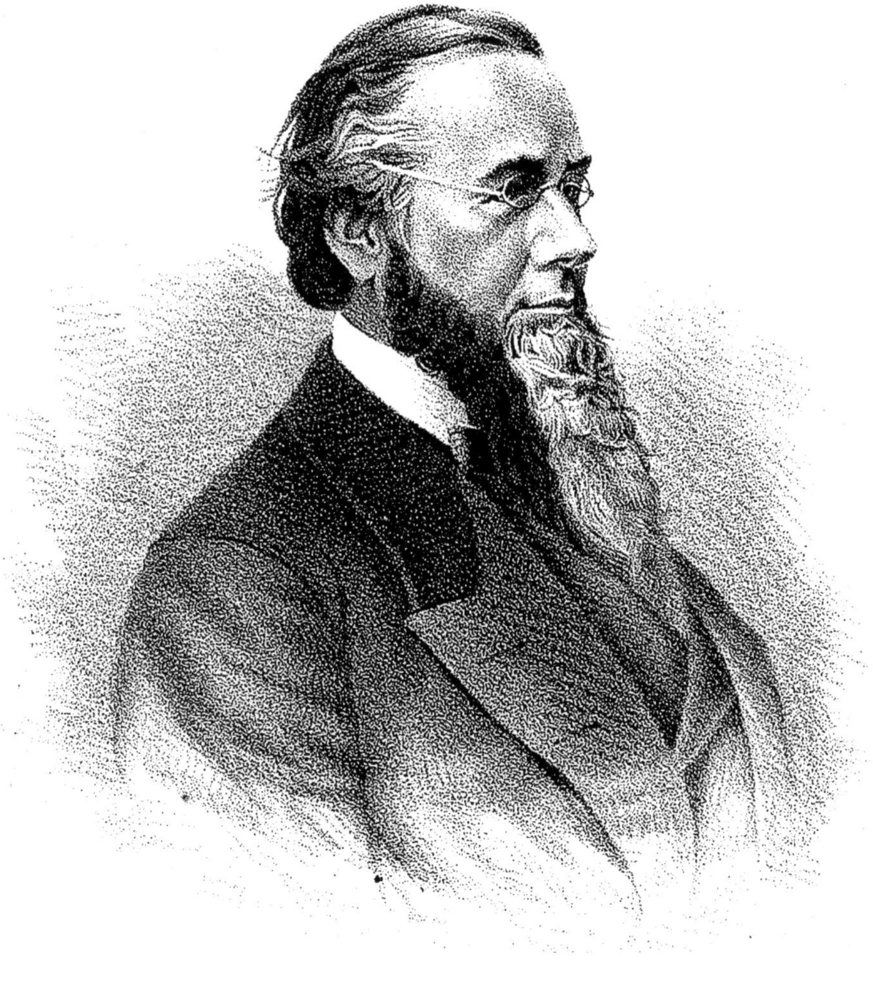

Edwin M. Stanton, president Lincoln's secretary of war during the Civil War. *Caldwell's* History of Belmont and Jefferson Counties.

and found instead Deuteronomy 20:1— "When thou goest out to battle against thine enemies, and seest horses, and chariots, and a people more than thou, be not afraid of them: for the LORD thy God is with thee, which brought thee up out of the land of Egypt." He preached for an hour on this text, whipping the regiment out of its panic.

Roused out of their fear and into their duty, the soldiers now cheered and huzzahed ("huzzah" would not turn into "hurrah" for another generation). Buchanan did not limit his zeal to sermons, though. He would not just pump the boys up, pat them on the back and send them into battle—he hopped on trusty old Punch and *led* the charge upriver to meet the supposed enemy host. After such a stirring moment, and such a build-up from an overenthusiastic storyteller, we almost regret the fact that there was no enemy to meet. The report had been false.

From "Free Schools" to Public to Parochial

There were imitators of Buchanan's academy right away. Bezaleel Wells himself raised subscriptions for an academy in 1818, which he built on south High Street, hiring Professor J.P. Miller to run it. This was the second school that Wells had provided his town. Samuel Ackerly began a private school in 1820, and Dr. John Scott one in 1830. While these private schools flourished, the publicly funded "Little Red Schoolhouse" failed to attract Steubenville's best scholars—in fact, it drew hardly any at all, despite the fact that it was the only school in town that did not charge tuition, being publicly supported.

Since the Reverend C.C. Beatty now had a decade's success with the Female Seminary, the businessmen of the town looked to him to solve this public education dilemma. James Means, who had just taken over the Phillips foundry, knew that the prosperity his industry would bring to Steubenville could support an admirable school system. So he called Beatty and other leaders together to organize a town board of education. On October 1, 1838, the board met to plan the raising of funds to build two new schools and to commission a study to find out why the public school was so underattended.

The report, issued two years later by Means and Dr. John Andrews, has been called by Steubenville historian J.B. Doyle "the Magna Carta of our local school system." Its findings were simple: the public had avoided the free school because they thought of it as a "poor school"; it became a stigma to send your child there, as if you couldn't afford a "better" school. The board began a public relations campaign to convince the people of Steubenville that their town schools would offer the best education available.

Two new brick buildings went up in 1840 at a cost of $2,000 each, easily raised by a small town tax. One building was located on the east side of South Fourth Street, just north of Slack, and the other on North Fourth, just north of Logan. The success of the board's public relations efforts can be gauged by the fact that the square, four-room schools were built to accommodate 250 students each, a total of 500, and that the enrollment on opening day in 1840 was 653. Rooms were rented to accommodate the extra students, and an addition was built for the north school the following year. The Means-

Andrews report had calculated a total of 1,336 school-aged children in 1840—though "school age" was defined as ages four to twenty-one, and by sixteen most boys were in a trade. Nevertheless, the numbers suggest that perhaps half of Steubenville's youth were still in private schools. However, the quality of the new schools began to draw more and more.

In 1853, Steubenville's African Methodist Episcopal Church on the corner of Third and South opened a school for Steubenville's African American children, supported by the board. Since this was a full century before *Brown v. the Board of Education*, we might look on this development as the beginning of segregated schooling in Steubenville. In starting a separate school, the board may have been more progressive than it seems from our century's standpoint. First, it was responding to the will of the leader of Steubenville's AME church, Reverend M.M. Clark, as well as founder of the congregation—the first AME church in the West—Bishop William Paul Quinn. Second, the board publicly declared its obligation to fund the African American school. Third, when it became obvious that "separate but equal" was not working in Steubenville education, the board desegregated the city schools—not in the 1950s, like the rest of the nation, but in 1883.

The Catholic parochial school system began in Steubenville in 1868 when Reverend W.T. Bigelow opened a Catholic elementary school in the basement of St. Peter's Roman Catholic Church on North Fourth Street. Father Bigelow had just been reassigned from duties in the archdiocesan office in Cincinnati as part of a restructuring that created the new Diocese of Columbus. Starting a school was one of his primary assignments; the teaching would be done by Dominican Sisters.

By 1879, the five rooms in the basement were full—there were now three hundred students in the parish school—and Father Bigelow was tasked with adding high school grades as well. He enlisted the aid of an Irish priest fresh out of seminary in Columbus, Reverend M.M.A. Hartnedy. Proving equally adept at real estate as at teaching high school science and math, Father Hartnedy acquired a property on the corner of Fifth and Slack Streets in 1884, which he immediately converted to a Catholic high school. Later it would become Holy Name Church. A gifted musician and a great Irish tenor, Father Hartnedy encouraged musical and dramatic productions in his high schools, and in 1892, for the 400th anniversary of the voyage of Columbus, Father H. wrote and directed a play on the subject, which became a popular school play elsewhere in America when published by the Columbus Club.

When a second restructuring of the Archdiocese of Cincinnati and the Diocese of Columbus created the new Diocese of Steubenville in 1945, the

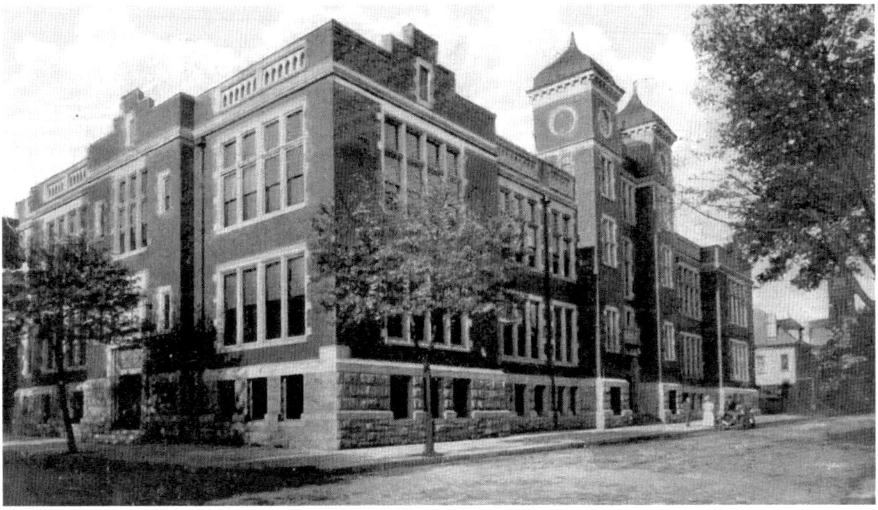

Wells High School, from a 1908 postcard. *Ohio Collection, Schiappa Library.*

first bishop of Steubenville, John King Mussio, acquired land in the west end of the city and built a modern high school, Steubenville Catholic Central, which graduated its first class in 1951.

Higher Education I: A Tale of Two Colleges

With the expansion of industry in Steubenville, business leaders felt the need for quality college-level instruction in Steubenville, but several attempts to begin a business college in Steubenville after the Civil War met with failure. Finally, in 1896, the last of these failing ventures hired a promising young business professor from Illinois named Joseph Terry Thompson. Arriving in Steubenville, Thompson was shocked to find that the school only had one student—and that the student only had one term to complete—with no new students in sight.

Convinced that Steubenville's business leaders were right—that this was the ideal place for a business college—Thompson took out a loan, bought the school, then occupying only three rooms in an office building at 185 North Fourth Street, and incorporated a new institution under the name of Steubenville Business College. Within a decade, the SBC covered the entire third floor of the building, and in 1902 it took over the Gill building at the corner of Fourth and Market, while continuing to keep the older building. In 1923, the college opened a third location, also at Fourth and Market.

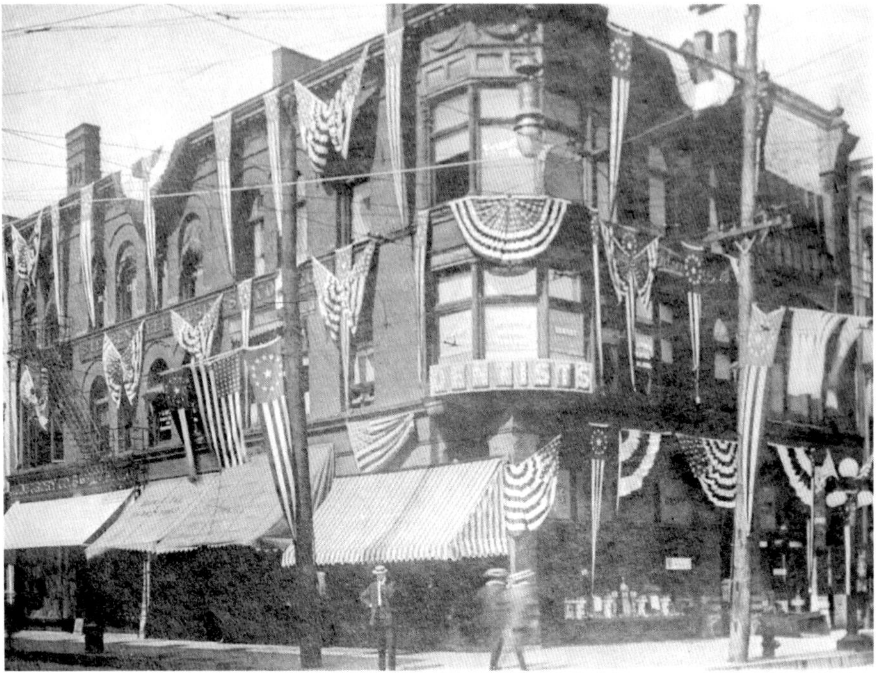

Steubenville Business College, Decoration Day, 1927. *Ohio Collection, Schiappa Library.*

In its first half-century, Steubenville Business College graduated more than ten thousand men and women. The key to Thompson's first success was his expertise with the typewriter, a relatively new item in 1896 but already essential to modern business. By the turn of the century, most of the typists in the city had been trained by Thompson, which in turn created a demand for more typists, bringing more students to the SBC and particularly bringing more women into the Steubenville workforce (and into the business college).

When J.T. Thompson died in 1951, his son, J. Vincent Thompson, CPA, who had established an accounting firm in Steubenville and taught accounting at the college, took it over and ran it successfully for another twenty years. Finally, however, competition from business departments in established four-year colleges—including the new College of Steubenville—forced the seventy-five-year-old institution to close its doors December 17, 1971. The younger Thompson kept ownership of the original offices at 185 North Fourth, where he continued to keep student records until his death in 2000.

In the meantime, college-level training of teachers was also taking place in Steubenville. In 1853, Superintendent of Steubenville Schools Thomas F. McGrew established a Teachers Institute in the city, which all city teachers had to attend at least two hours a week. This was not the same as a teachers' college or "normal school," but clearly McGrew had ambitions in that direction. Those ambitions were not realized, however, for another fifty years. In 1907, the new superintendent, Dr. Robert L. Erwin, opened the City Normal School, a one-year program with transfer credits accepted by all two- and four-year teachers' colleges. After the First World War, Dr. Erwin expanded the curriculum and began working toward certification to turn City Normal into a junior college. Unfortunately, the Great Depression came along, and instead of expanding, City Normal closed forever in 1932. Steubenville would have to wait another thirty-six years to get its own two-year college.

Higher Education II: A Tale of Two More Colleges

When the Roman Catholic Diocese of Steubenville was formed in 1945, and its first bishop, John King Mussio, created Steubenville Catholic Central High School, he also hoped to start a Catholic college. Hundreds of young men were returning to Steubenville from the Second World War, and the Serviceman Readjustment Act of 1944—commonly known as the "GI Bill"—made tuition money available to them. College enrollments were swelling; it was a good time to start a college.

Of all the orders of Catholic priests, the one most associated with higher education was the Society of Jesus—the Jesuits. Quite naturally, then, Bishop Mussio went to them first. Certainly, the order's representative told the new bishop. We would be delighted to start a new Jesuit college in Steubenville. All we need is $1 million up front, and we'll start tomorrow.

A million. If they meant prayers, we're okay. If they meant dollars, they've got to be kidding. Steubenville was indeed booming in the mid-'40s: the wartime needs for steel kept Steubenville's economy rolling. The city had just hit its peak population in 1940 at 37,651 and would soon begin its decline. But $1 million? In the twenty-first century, $1 million may not seem like much, but as Senator Everett Dirksen would say, in 1945, $1 million was "real money."

Then Bishop Mussio remembered the mendicant orders in the church, the "begging" orders who took a vow of poverty. If you had to build a college with no resources, who better to go to than priests who are used to working with nothing? The bishop knew that the Franciscans of the Third Order Regular had started a college in Loretto, Pennsylvania, a century earlier. Maybe they would only need $0.5 million.

Well, the Franciscans were delighted with the offer to start a college and convinced Bishop Mussio that they could get the start-up capital the same way that St. Francis had: by begging. Father Daniel Egan and Father Regius Stafford were sent to Steubenville to work out the logistics. With no money from the diocese, they went right to the banks and bought three buildings with a little more than a third of that million; $348,000 bought three buildings in downtown Steubenville.

The former Knights of Pythias building on Washington Street became the main academic building of what would become known as the College of Steubenville. Two houses on North Fourth Street became the friary (to house the Franciscans who would supply the human capital for the college) and the biology building. Instead of lamenting the dispersed nature of such an arrangement, the first professors and students proudly spoke of a "North Campus" and "Main Campus"—surrounded by downtown Steubenville.

On opening day, in September 1946, there were 251 men and 7 women lined up to take courses. By 1950, a third of the students were female; after 1970, female students would be in the majority (as in most U.S. colleges). Most of the men in those first years were soldiers on the GI Bill. By the start of the new decade, the young college had gone through its first four-year cycle and was ready to graduate its first class, the 70 students of the class of 1951. It would be another decade, 1960, before that number was equaled. Growth was slow.

A small college in the 1950s could not hope to attract top scholars to its faculty. However, Dr. John Carrigg, who joined the faculty in the late 1940s and would see the College of Steubenville through half a century of growth, remembers one side effect of the Cold War that brought some of the best academic minds in Europe to Steubenville. The Eisenhower administration had talked about the "brain drain," the rush of two World War II allies, the United States and the USSR, to outdo each other in snapping up the greatest minds, particularly scientific minds, of Europe.

When it became clear that all of eastern Europe was turning into a client state of the Soviets, many academics defected to the West. Dr. Carrigg's retrospective for the university's fiftieth anniversary in 1996 listed the great European professors who came to the College of Steubenville in the mid-1950s: Dr. Edward Gora, physics; Dr. Michael Dudra, economics; Dr. Bohdan Lonchyna, linguistics; Dr. Joseph Felicijan, history; Dr. Leonida Jurgens, sociology; and Dr. Kazys Pakstas, geography. For a small Midwest college to have that many PhDs in the 1950s was unheard of.

The enrollment growth seen in the late 1960s throughout U.S. colleges helped Steubenville as well. In 1961, construction began on a new campus

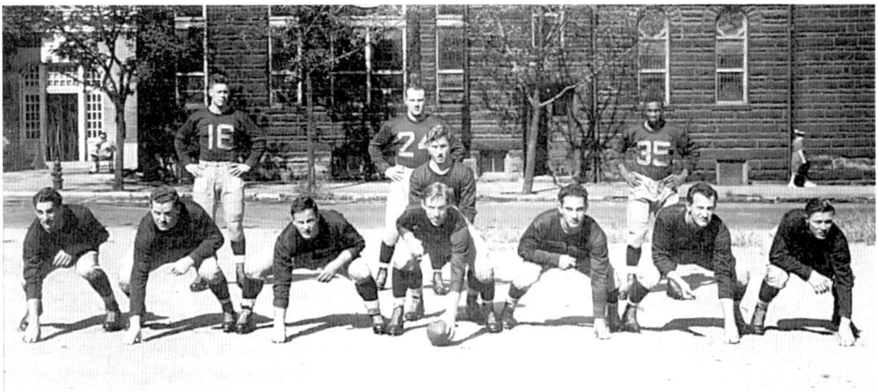

The College of Steubenville football team, pre-1951. *Franciscan University of Steubenville.*

on the hilltop overlooking downtown Steubenville, but the downturn in the early 1970s also hit the College of Steubenville and nearly did it in. In 1970, the college's enrollment peaked at 1,333. By the end of the decade, enrollment would be nearly half that (735 in 1978). In 1974, the Carnegie Institute studied this nationwide problem, producing a list of five hundred small colleges most likely to fail within five years. The College of Steubenville was on that list. One of its dorms was listed for sale in the Steubenville *Herald Star*.

The Franciscans, who had started with nothing, knew how to respond to hard times. They simply kept faith. When the college's fourth president, Father Michael Scanlan, accepted the reins of a nearly defunct college, he proclaimed that if the College of Steubenville were to come to an end, it would come to an end true to the spiritual values on which it was founded. That summer the university began a series of summer conferences for priests to share those values. As the summer conferences expanded, word of mouth from the participants had more and more Catholics nationwide thinking of Steubenville as the place to get a good Catholic education.

As enrollments rebounded, the college added graduate programs, attaining university status in 1980. Beginning as essentially a "commuter college," with most of its students from southeast Ohio or western Pennsylvania, the University of Steubenville began the 1980s as a destination of choice for students in all fifty states and forty-four foreign countries. In remembering its Franciscan beginnings ("Franciscan" became part of its corporate name in 1984), the university did not forget its Steubenville beginnings. In the twenty-first century, Ohio remained the number one state of origin for its students.

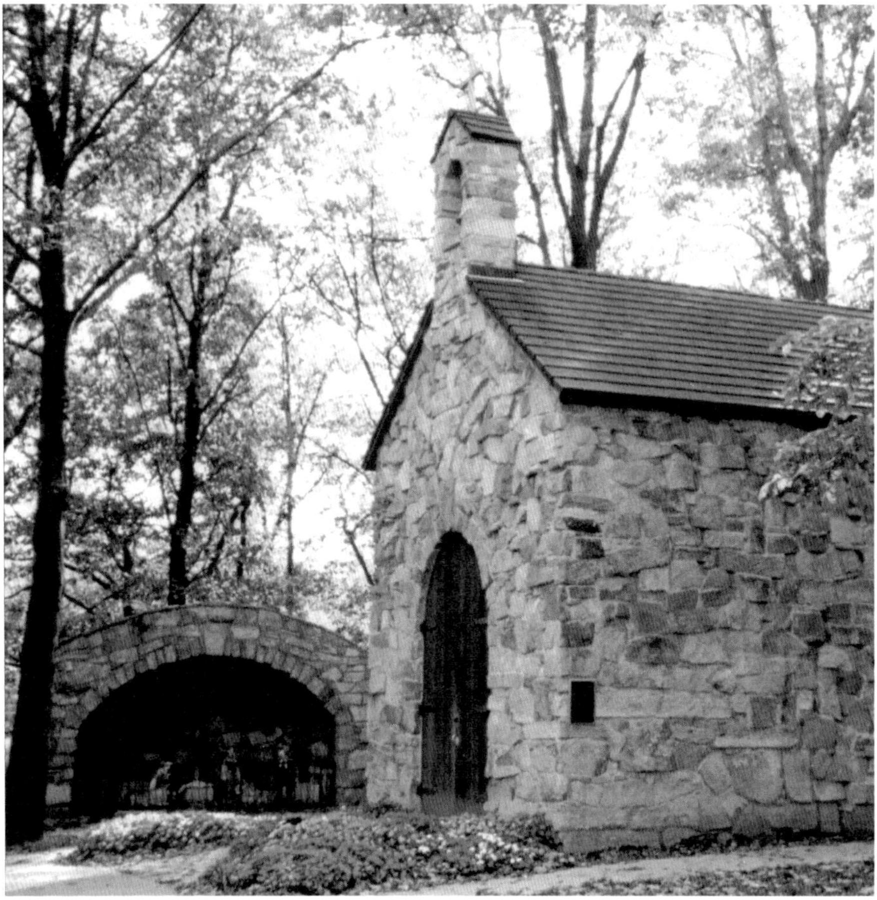

The Portiuncula, a reproduction of the thirteenth-century chapel rebuilt by St. Francis, located on the campus of Franciscan University of Steubenville and named as an official pilgrimage site by the Vatican in 2009. *Franciscan University of Steubenville.*

During the latter half of the development of Franciscan University of Steubenville, another college was born in the west end of the city. In the mid-1960s, the continuing prosperity of steelmaking in the Ohio Valley also created a need for a higher degree of technical education in the workforce. A Battelle Institute study completed on October 29, 1965, concluded that Steubenville and Jefferson County had a distinct need for postsecondary technical education.

Jefferson County was looking to get in on the national trend of counties in urban areas supporting technical and community colleges. At the same time, counties were getting out of the orphanage and nursing home businesses.

On September 16, 1966, the Jefferson County Home for the Aged on Sunset Boulevard was deemed no longer required for public use, and so a new county entity, the Jefferson County Technical Institute, was recognized by the Ohio Technical Institute Board of Regents. The county's voters showed their support by passing a one-mill, ten-year levy to support the new institute two months later.

The following fall, ground was broken at the former Home for the Aged, and after a year of construction, "Jeff Tech" opened its doors to 320 students on September 23, 1968. Two-year associate degree programs were available in business, public service, engineering, health technologies and secretarial science.

The first decade of Jefferson Technical Institute saw stable enrollments at a time when college enrollments were declining. In 1976, the voters approved an extension of the tax levy supporting the institute, and the following year the school's board of trustees set its sights on achieving what the City Normal School had failed to do forty years earlier: bringing a true junior college to Steubenville.

In 1977, the Ohio Board of Regents approved a name change to Jefferson Technical College, but there was little change in curriculum. After a third ten-year levy was passed in 1986, however, plans to expand the course offerings went forward. In 1992, the board approved a Jefferson County citizens committee to effect the change; even to hire teachers in subjects unrelated to their tech-school curriculum—such as history, English or psychology—required state approval.

In October 1993, the state attorney general approved a transfer of the levy from tech to community college, and the following September the Ohio Board of Regents approved the curriculum change. In 1995, the college accrediting agency, the North Central Association, approved two new degree programs, Associate of Arts and Associate of Sciences, and Steubenville finally had its own community college.

In 2005, the new community college obtained the building and grounds vacated by its neighbor, American Electric Power, and converted the building to the Pugliese Training Center for Workforce and Community Outreach. The new building houses six classrooms, a café and conference facilities. Through the Enterprise Ohio Network, JCC became a center for workforce retraining as local industries adjust to a changing economy. The college customizes employee training to suit employers' needs.

JCC also became a center for Microsoft Office computer software certification; a police academy approved by the Ohio Attorney General's Office; and professional development with continuing education units (CEU)

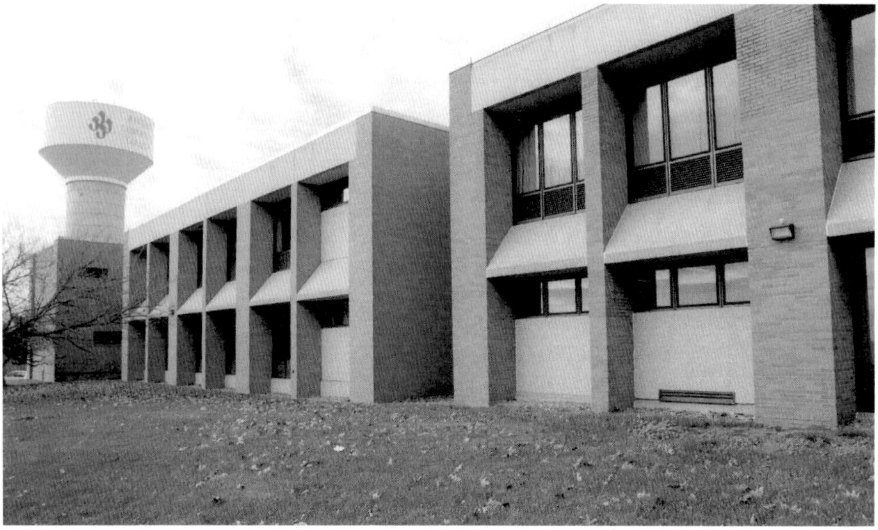

Jefferson Community College, with the JCC logo on the city water tower. *Ohio Collection, Schiappa Library.*

in the fields of insurance, medicine, dentistry, radiology, cosmetology and education. Professional offices throughout the Ohio Valley became staffed with JCC graduates.

By the time Jefferson Community College celebrated its fortieth anniversary in 2008, 30,368 enrolled students had passed through its doors. With state funding providing more than 40 percent of its budget, and county support continuing, "Jeff Com" in the first decade of the twenty-first century was able to offer free tuition to qualified local students through its "Horizon Grants."

PART V

Stores and Skyscrapers: The Look of Downtown

Where Did Steubenville Shop?

I am as shopping impaired as the next American male, but I have to admit that one of the first things I think about when trying to picture everyday life in the Steubenville of old is, "Where did everyone shop?" Certainly America was less of a consumer culture in 1797 than it is today, and Steubenville was a frontier town, but it *was* a town and not a rural settlement. Elsewhere in the county, settlers made or grew or traded for most of the things that they needed and would only periodically go into town for supplies—but when they did, that "town" was Steubenville. The people who lived in Steubenville probably went to market almost daily.

When he first laid out the town in 1797, Bezaleel Wells made a "town square" the center, intending it to become a marketplace. As already stated, shops began to line the aptly named Market Street in the first year of the town's settlement. Before 1800, the first three buildings on Third Street going north from Market were all general stores (Wilson's, Hale's and Means's), and the next two were taverns. The first building on Third on the south side of Market was also a general store.

Then, with the new century, a pair of Virginia swells by the names of Robert and James Hening blew into town, sporting the newest fashions from Philadelphia, and established a clothing store on Market Street that catered to fashionable gentlemen. Every spring Robert would travel to Philadelphia, buy the latest in men's wear and bring it back to Steubenville. Cutting a fine figure himself, he became his own model, strolling Market Street in the newest style, hoping that every man would want something like it.

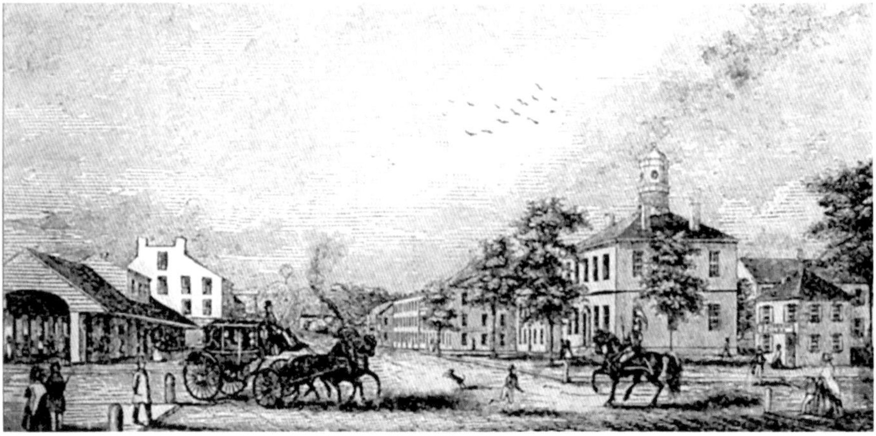

Steubenville Public Square, 1846. The Jefferson County Courthouse on the right was built in 1808, the Market House at left in 1809. *Ohio Collection, Schiappa Library.*

In the centennial edition of the Steubenville *Herald* in 1897, Mrs. Ida Means wrote a retrospective in which she described Mr. Hening's attire (though the description must have been handed down to her by elders with clearer memories of 1805): "white silk hat, blue broadcloth coat, linen frills, small clothes, and shoes of marvelous shine."

The Market Square was also a market in the Old World sense. Jefferson County farmers would bring their produce there to sell to all comers. In 1812, the city built a market building with public funds. The overhanging roof allowed even the tallest wagons to unload their contents, and draymen and teamsters soon crowded the foot of Market Street, at the river, to unload barges and keelboats and haul their contents two blocks uphill to the market house.

The large, single-building department store was a post–Civil War phenomenon. In Steubenville, however, many merchants of the first half of the nineteenth century anticipated the American trend toward "bigger is better" by expanding to multiple locations in the city. One of the first of such Steubenville entrepreneurs was a young fruit farmer named John D. Slack. In the early 1820s (when he was himself in his early twenties), Slack started a nursery in a grove just south of what was then the city limits—aptly named South Street.

An experimenter in grafting and crossbreeding fruit trees, Slack gave the farms of the upper Ohio Valley many of its distinctive varieties of apples—most of which no longer exist in an era of shrinking biodiversity. He sold saplings, seed and apples—plenty of apples. When customers complained about having to negotiate the dirt road to his orchard for

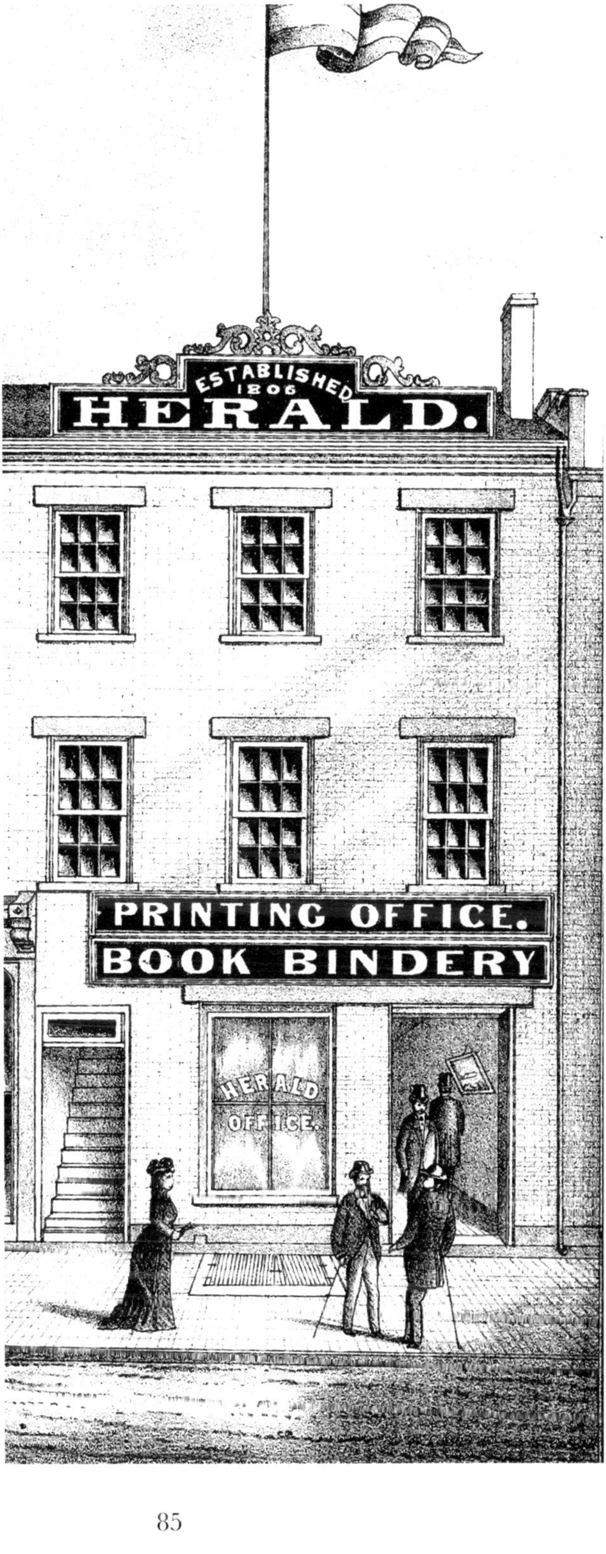

The *Western Herald* of 1806 became the *Steubenville Herald* in this 1880 engraving, and it is still published as the *Herald Star*. *Caldwell's* History of Belmont and Jefferson Counties.

his merchandise (it would soon be improved and named, naturally, Slack Street), he decided, like a good businessman, to meet them where they were. By 1830, he had three locations in Steubenville, selling seed, produce (a complete grocery line, in fact) and gardening supplies.

In 1832, Slack, by this time an expert landscaper, transformed the grove south of the city into a pleasure park billed as "Slack's Linden Hill Gardens." Drive by the downtown branch of the Steubenville Library today, and you are in the heart of what was once Slack's Gardens—filled with roses and groves of trees—and it was the number one courtship spot in Steubenville in the 1830s. When friends told him that his homemade ice cream was the best in Steubenville, Slack opened a café in the gardens to feature his frozen treat, and even more young people flocked to the park.

As Steubenville expanded, it absorbed Slack's Gardens. It is now a two-block wedge of the city bounded by Slack and Fourth Streets and the railroad tracks. One later landscaping feat of Slack's still survives, though certainly much changed in more than a century and a half: Steubenville's Union Cemetery, which Slack helped design in 1853.

Steubenville's Hening brothers had been ahead of their time in marketing premade clothing in 1805, when most clothing not made in the home was made to order by merchant tailors. It stands to reason, though, that a town whose leading industry was textiles would be ahead of the curve when it came to premade fashion. So it was that Steubenville's first department store began as a clothing store.

In 1847, Edward Frohman, later joined by his brother, Morris, opened a store that would soon be *the* fashionable place to shop in Steubenville. The Frohmans moved several times in its first few years, but the spot they finally settled on in 1852—the southeast corner of Third and Market—had been mercantile grounds since 1798, when Samuel Hunter set up his general store there. The future of retail on that spot, however, would belong to a young man named Jones Munker, who hired on as a clerk at Frohman's in February 1859. Three years later he became a partner in the firm and, in 1867, sole proprietor of what would now be known as Munker's—it would no longer be simply a clothing store or simply a storefront.

For the next quarter century, Jones Munker would buy up any property on his block that became available as he expanded his merchandise to include "domestic goods" (houseware items) and dry goods. Munker's continued to be primarily a clothing store, but even that became departmentalized, with a different store front for children's clothes, "gent's furnishings," hats, shoes and the "ladies' department," which included clothing, millinery, lace, hosiery and "fancy goods."

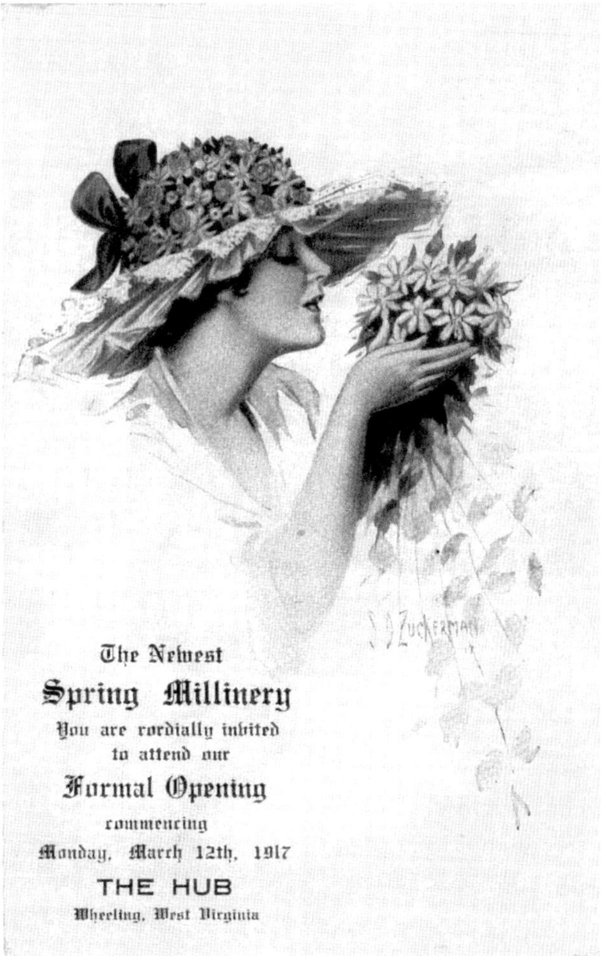

Ad card for spring millinery fashions at the Hub, 1917, sent to regular customers. *Ohio Collection, Schiappa Library.*

In 1891, Munker bought the last property on the block and tore them all down to make way for a single three-story palace to house his department store—with seventeen-foot ceilings on the first floor (children's and ladies' clothes and hats), fourteen on the second (tailoring and men's clothing) and twelve on the third (warehouse and storage)—even the basement (domestic goods) had nine-foot ceilings.

Yet with all that space, Munker's did not have the biggest floor space in Steubenville at the end of the nineteenth century. That honor belonged to Winfield Scott, whose history paralleled Munker's. Coming to Steubenville the same year as Munker's predecessor, Frohman (1847), William Scott started a general store on South Fourth. Moving across Market Street to

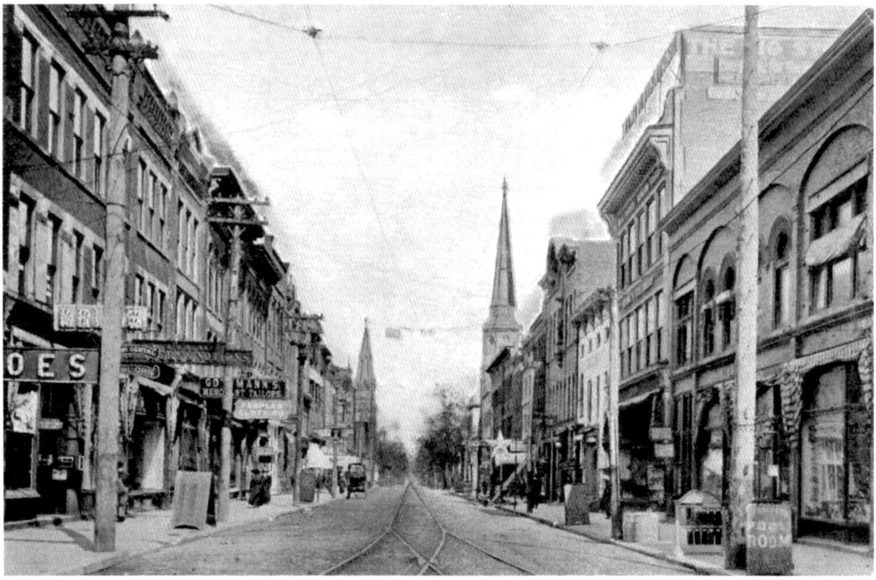

North Fourth Street, circa 1918. The tallest building on the right is Winfield Scott, Son, & Co.'s Big Store. *Ohio Collection, Schiappa Library.*

North Fourth in 1850, Scott took over an entire three-story building, dubbed it the "Big Store" and began Steubenville's version of the pursuit of bigger and better. When William Scott retired in 1872, the firm took on his son's name (Winfield Scott), and until the turn of the century, Scott's "Big Store" had more floor space than any other store in eastern Ohio.

By 1900, however, the biggest department store in Steubenville was Sulzbacher's. Isadore Sulzbacher came from Germany to New York at age fourteen. His father was a dry goods merchant, but instead of teaching him the business, he apprenticed young Izzy to a variety of New York retailers. This experience really paid off in Steubenville, where he sold, well, everything. His last employment before going into business for himself was in lace and embroidery, so when he came to set up shop in Steubenville in 1888, he dealt in ladies' fashions. By the mid-1890s he had taken over all four floors of the Cochran Building opposite city hall on Market and was renting warehouse space elsewhere.

Thus, when the National Exchange Bank opened its new five-story headquarters in 1905 and called it "Steubenville's First Skyscraper"—we'll get to that story later—Sulzbacher was first in line to lease space. In fact, he signed a ten-year lease on the basement the moment the National Exchange announced its new building project, and by opening day he had the first and second floors

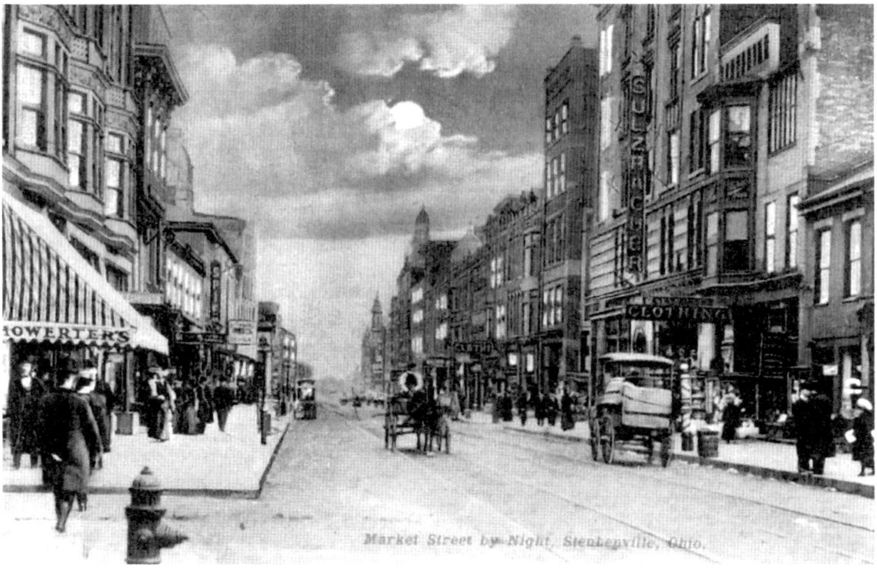

Market Street circa 1900, with Sulzbacher's Department Store at right, Spies Jewelers at left. *Ohio Collection, Schiappa Library.*

as well—only three floors, but each one twice as spacious as his former location, so that the new Sulzbacher's had twelve thousand feet of floor space.

At any of its locations, Sulzbacher's at the turn of the last century was a sight to see. Mr. Sulzbacher installed rail systems to deliver orders and other paperwork from one department to another, anticipating the pneumatic delivery systems that the banks (and later Sulzbacher himself) would introduce to Steubenville. Housewares were found in the basement, the first floor dry goods and notions and the second floor ladies' wear and millinery. Here is where Sulzbacher's experience in New York's garment industry paid off. While hats were sold on the second floor, they were made on the third—which means that Steubenville's most fashionable ladies had their hats made to order. Also, since Sulzbacher had worked with the leading dress-pattern maker in New York—Butterick's—he was the exclusive Steubenville distributor of the patterns.

The Hub: 1904–1980

Perhaps the biggest shift in the history of American retailing was the exodus of urban downtown shoppers to the suburban malls. Steubenville was no

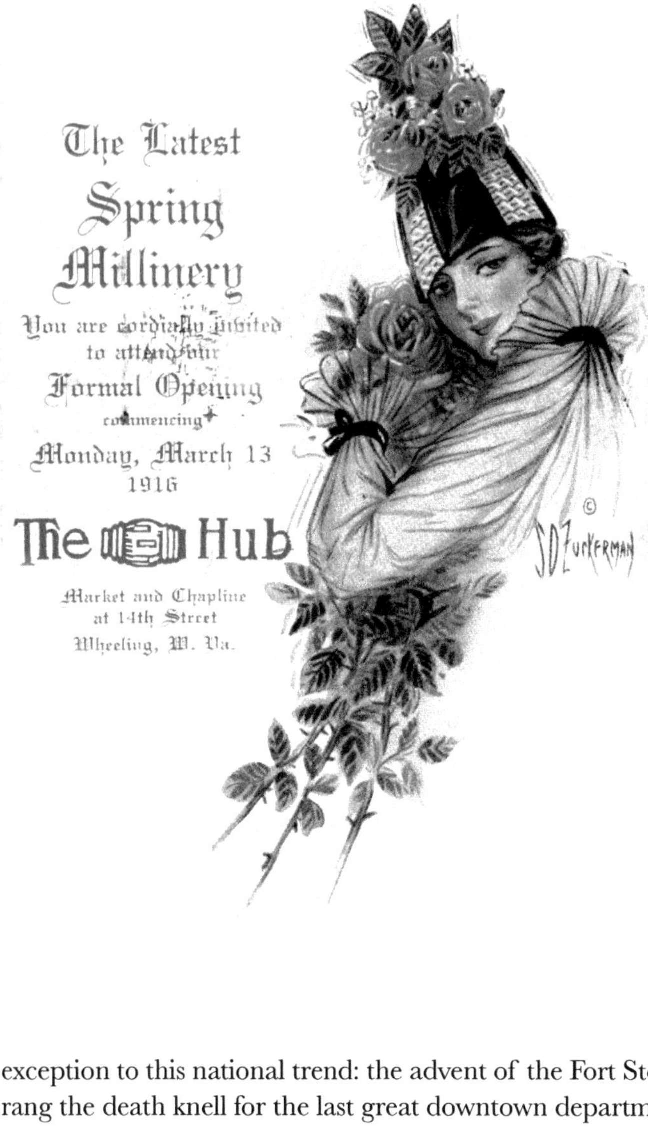

Ad card for the spring of 1916 from the Hub. *Ohio Collection, Schiappa Library*.

exception to this national trend: the advent of the Fort Steuben Mall in 1974 rang the death knell for the last great downtown department store, the Hub.

The Hub. The store's name told the story. For seventy-six years this institution was indeed the center not just of shopping but also of social activity in downtown Steubenville. Certainly, there was a time when the name "Hub" was an exaggeration or wishful thinking. When Mone Anathan and his brother, Simon, opened the store on the southwest corner of Fifth and Market on April 9, 1904, it was a simple (though elegant) men's clothing store. Two years later, business was brisk enough to support the Anathans' other two brothers, Eugene and Louis, and the four brothers needed more space.

In 1909, the Hub took over the entire basement floor of what was then known as the Johnson building, across the street on the northwest corner of Fifth and Market. From men's clothing it expanded to women's and children's fashions and then housewares, and soon it was rivaling Sulzbacher's as a "notions" or department store.

By 1916, the Anathan brothers had filled the entire building—the basement where they had started and both upper floors. The only place to expand was up. On April 19, 1917, they awarded a contract for an ambitious addition: extra floors, state-of-the-art elevators, pneumatic message systems and a new terra-cotta façade. Unfortunately, that big announcement was overshadowed by other news that would delay the renovation. Less than two weeks earlier, the United States entered the First World War. Construction projects unrelated to the war effort were put on hold. Then, with the peace a year and a half later, the steel industry was hit with massive strikes, and construction materials were hard to get.

Thus, it was May 15, 1922, before the construction began, but it was finished almost immediately. On June 3, 1922, ads in all four Steubenville papers announced "The Greatest Sale in the History of Steubenville." The new and improved Hub had arrived.

This new four-story full-city block is the Hub that pre-1980 residents of Steubenville remember fondly. Those who came later (including the author) can think of the recreation of 1940s Higbees in the iconic film *A Christmas Story* and get the idea of what the Hub was to Steubenville and the entire Ohio Valley. Or perhaps not fully. Because the Hub was more than just a big city department store in a small city. Yes, it had all the departments (twenty-seven of them, not counting service departments like credit and gift-wrapping), connected by pneumatic tubes in which orders could be sent. Yes, it had, at its peak, 325 employees. But it also had, according to its nostalgic employees, a sense of customer service that, like so many aspects of the past, was not appreciated until it was gone.

"Customer service" is a cliché, and it is an article of faith among the American consumer that it was always better in the past than it is now. A look at some of the Hub's practices should be sufficient proof that the Hub was someplace special, even for its time. For one thing, the Anathans seemed to understand the gender politics of merchandizing. In 1922, the expectation was that men were the breadwinners and women did the shopping. Even in the supposedly progressive twenty-first century, social scientists observe that the male human, for the most part, still lacks that crucial shopping gene.

Long before the human marketing genome was mapped, however, the Anathans had found ways to bring the Steubenville male into the Hub. One was by bringing that bastion of male mystery, the barbershop, into the Hub. In fact, when Dean Martin was growing up in Steubenville, his father, Guy Crocetti, leased the barbershop in the Hub. A second tactic was developed at Christmastime. The Anathans lamented the fundamental inequity that the shopping-impaired male brought to Christmas giving. Wives and girlfriends and sisters would begin their consumer research, if not their gift shopping, right after Thanksgiving. Husbands and boyfriends and brothers would start right after dinner on Christmas Eve.

The Hub responded to this inequity by advertizing "Men's Night" early enough in the Christmas season to avoid the rush. Imagine it: the whole Hub an extended barbershop or boys' treehouse, where a guy could meet his poker buddies, who understood the pressure of having to find something she would like. Sure, there might be a few women around, so it still wasn't safe to spit or scratch yourself. You knew that you were surrounded by guys who were just as stymied as you by the mysteries of feminine gifting.

But when he found the perfect gift, Joe Steubenville was not abandoned by the Anathans. They knew they had to offer free gift-wrapping, of course, since they noticed that some of their male customers still had mangled Scotch tape remnants from last Christmas on their thumbs. Hot snacks and drinks in the tearoom were a must. They also knew that, because Steubenville's women had already been shopping for a while, they had garnered the best gift-hiding places in the home. So the sales clerks on Men's Night were trained to promote two services: gift storage (men could leave their wrapped and labeled gifts at the store until Christmas Eve) and, for the professional men, office delivery. The Hub would sneak wrapped gifts into men's offices, where they would be safe until Christmas.

There was also a girls' night out, though. "Ladies' Night" at Christmastime was designed to offer Madame maximum contact with merchandise. If there was no one to watch Junior or Suzie Q, the tearoom became a game room, where mothers were encouraged to leave their children for supervised play.

The Great Skyscraper Race

What is the tallest building in Steubenville? That's easy. Since 1922 it has been the Steubenville Bank and Trust Building, twelve stories tall. When we consider that, at that time, New York boasted the Singer Building at forty-seven floors, the Met Life Tower at fifty and the Woolworth Building at fifty-seven, it may seem absurd to call a mere dozen stories a "skyscraper." Nobody uses that word for any building in Steubenville today. But nearly a

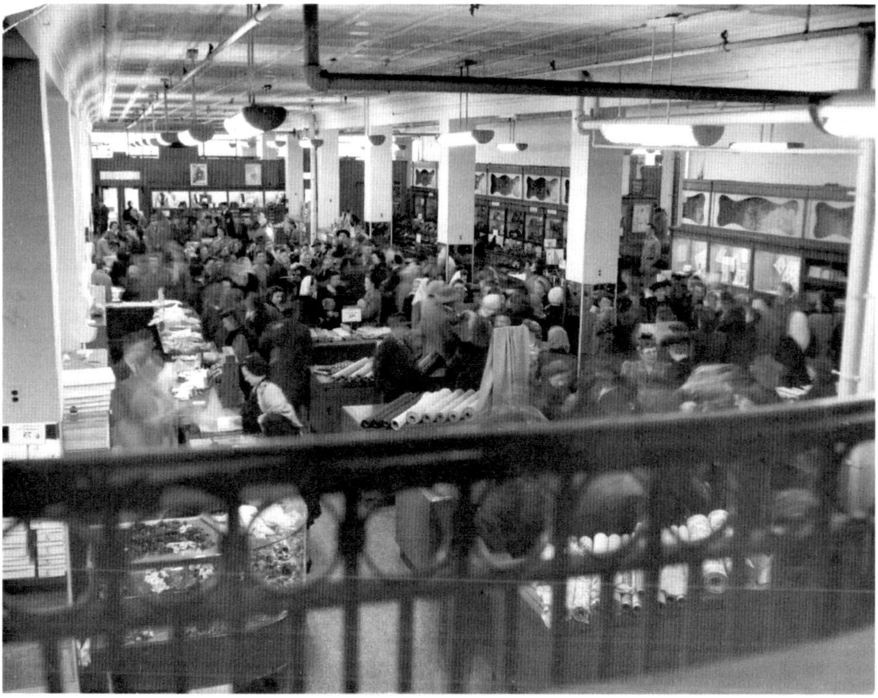

Sale at the Hub, mid-1940s. *Ohio Collection, Schiappa Library.*

century ago, three rival Steubenville banks vied to have the tallest building in the city, and all three were called "skyscrapers"—at least locally.

In the longest-standing architectural usage of the term, a building need not meet a height requirement to be called a skyscraper. The first building to receive that term, Chicago's Home Insurance Building (1885), was only ten stories high. Architects still apply the term to buildings that size if they rise above the surrounding architecture, as Steubenville's tallest buildings do. Steubenville's tallest edifices do not, however, dominate the skyline, because Steubenville doesn't really have a skyline. Buildings twice as high as the city's highest would still be dwarfed by the hills that look down on downtown Steubenville.

In Steubenville, though, the impulse to have skyscrapers—if the reader can accept that term—was not aimed at the skyline. It was sheer one-upmanship on the part of three local banks: the National Exchange Bank, the Union Savings Bank and the Steubenville Bank and Trust—though the moment the SB&T moved into the building, it merged with the National Exchange. So you could say that the race came down to two banks.

The National Exchange started the competition, and it was the first to claim the title "skyscraper." On October 9, 1903, before the contract to

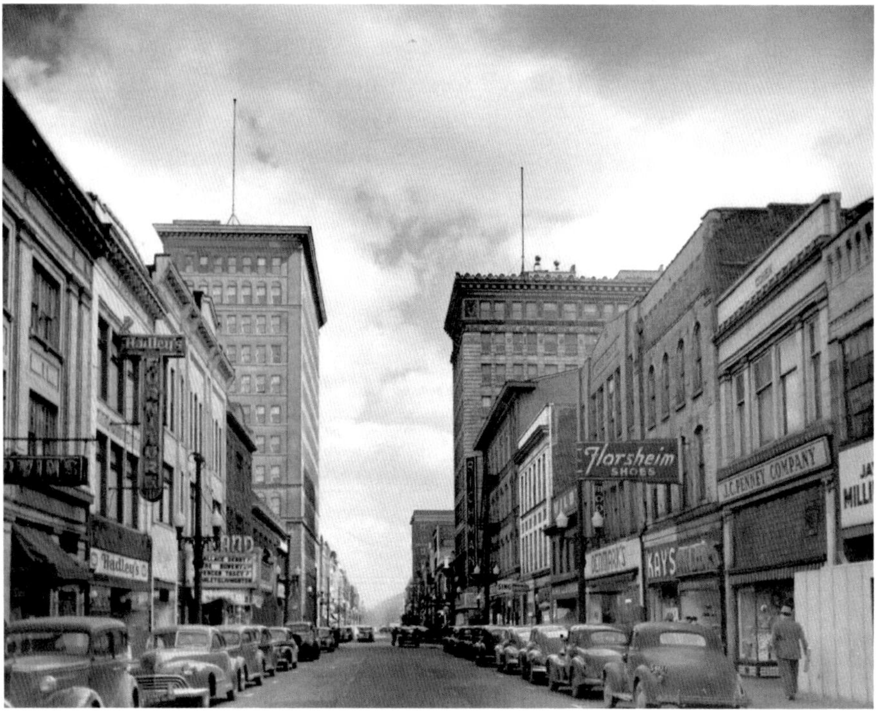

Steubenville's two "skyscrapers" in 1947: the National Exchange Building (left) and the Sinclair Building (right). *Ohio Collection, Schiappa Library.*

build the new National Exchange Building was even signed, the Steubenville *Herald Star* was already calling the proposed building "Steubenville's first sky scraper." When it opened on September 11, 1905, it was only five stories tall—a mere sprout by big city standards—but each floor had high ceilings, so that, as the *Herald Star* reported, it was equivalent to a seven-story building.

The *Herald Star* went on for 1,500 words describing the interior splendor of the building. The heavy steel vaults, the "rich Pavanozza marble and San Domingo mahogany," the safety deposit boxes and the pneumatic mail tubes "for the first time introduced to this city in the new building"—all evoked the most tremendous enthusiasm. But the article also served notice that the skyscraper competition had begun. "The bank," it said, "has set an example to the wealthy property holders and business houses of Steubenville to follow in the erection of buildings."

Follow they did. The press and the people of Steubenville were fired with architectural pride, and they wanted their city to be able to boast of skyscrapers "as fine as any in Pittsburgh." Appealing to Pittsburgh as a model was not just a function of its proximity to Steubenville. Pittsburgh's steel magnate, Andrew Carnegie—who had in his youth served as a messenger boy in Steubenville—understood that there should be a natural affinity between Pittsburgh and the new phenomenon of tall buildings in Chicago and New York. The reason was steel.

While Steubenville steel makers were justly proud of their city's role in the industry, they also knew that they were part of a region in which steel making was inevitable, since both the coal and the river were here. Carnegie knew that it was the steel his companies forged that made the new architecture possible. Load-bearing masonry has a height limit. At only nine stories, Philadelphia's city hall (begun 1871, finished 1901) remained the world's tallest load-bearing structure through most of the skyscraper era. "The Chicago skeleton" of the new skyscrapers —Pittsburgh-forged steel beams—took away those height limitations. In 1895, Carnegie joined the select group of skyscraper-builders with Pittsburgh's Carnegie Steel Building.

Steubenville's own Carnegie wannabe, the Union Deposit Bank's Dohrman J. Sinclair, understood that steel-frame buildings should be at home in Steubenville. Like Carnegie, he belonged to a dying breed of businessmen who came up in a sort of apprenticeship system. While Steubenville's other future bank presidents were setting their sights on Ivy League colleges, Sinclair was already banking. In 1873, when he was only thirteen, he was, as Carnegie had been, a Steubenville office boy at the Union Deposit. Sinclair was no street kid who hit it big, though, like Carnegie; his great-uncle Horatio Gates Garrett had started the bank in 1848, at first just as a security service, since he owned the only steel safe west of the Alleghenies.

When Garrett retired in 1887, his great-nephew bought Garrett's interest in the bank and moved it toward the twentieth century. As a major conduit of business capital in the Ohio Valley, Sinclair began working on local steel companies like La Belle Ironworks in Wheeling to take over the Jefferson Ironworks in Steubenville. That close relationship to local steel was the first criterion for another Steubenville skyscraper. In 1890, La Belle came to Steubenville.

The second step was convincing the bank's trustees that the pre Civil War building that was their home was no longer suitable. In 1892, they demolished the old building and built a new bank in its place. Only three stories tall (though the top and bottom floors had high ceilings), it was not even as big as the National Exchange building that would, a decade later, claim the title of Steubenville's first skyscraper. But Sinclair wasn't done building yet.

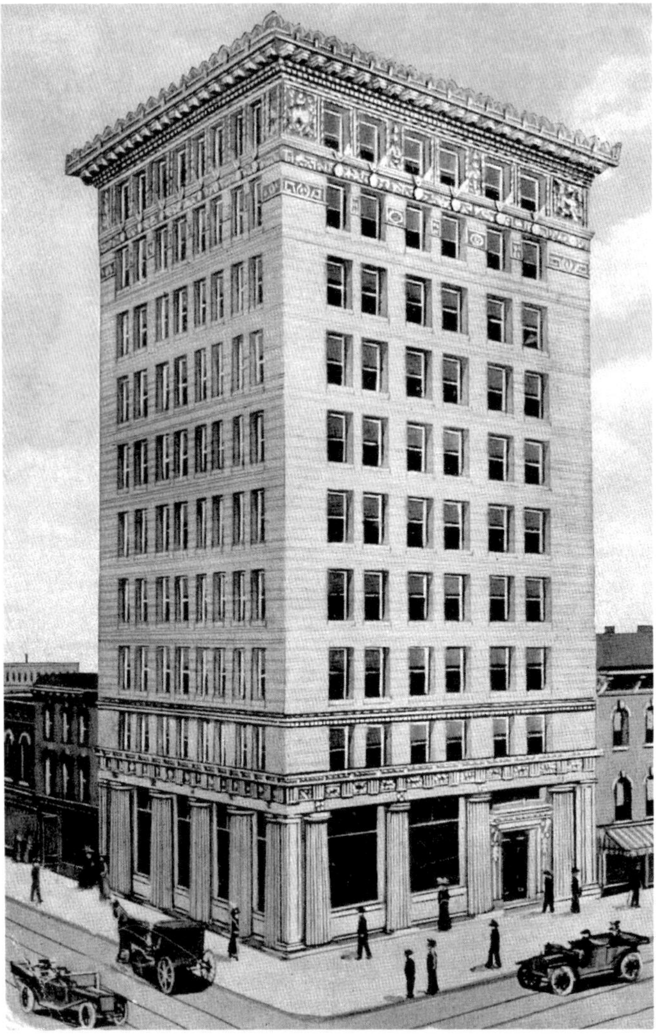

The Sinclair Building, shortly after its completion in 1915. Until surpassed by the First National Bank in 1922, it was Steubenville's tallest. *Ohio Collection, Schiappa Library.*

Sinclair knew that to leap into the twentieth century, Steubenville would need major overhauls of infrastructure. By investing in an electric trolley system and running it up to the hills overlooking Steubenville, Sinclair (and other investors) made possible housing developments like Pleasant Heights and La Belle View, both designed (as the La Belle name suggests) to house the hundreds of new workers that La Belle—and the Pope Tin Mill, another coup attributed to Sinclair—drew to Steubenville. In fact, the trolleys hauled the building materials to the top of the hill for the building project.

It was in the middle of that boom that the National Exchange Bank built its "skyscraper." Within a decade, though, Sinclair's would dwarf it.

In 1910, he announced plans for a new ten-story steel-and-concrete home for the Union Deposit. Work began January 28, 1914, and on August 11, 1915, it was finally opened. The celebration was muted by the fact that the day before, Dohrman J. Sinclair had been struck by an oncoming train and killed.

However, his Union Savings Bank building—the name was changed in a reincorporation of the new building—was soon rechristened the Sinclair Building, and so it remains. It would be the tallest building in Steubenville for only seven years, when it was topped—by two stories—by the First National Bank Bulding (now Chase). Completed in 1922, the First National had only one claim to fame: being taller than the Sinclair Building. Forgotten were the claims of a five-story shrimp like the National Exchange. When Steubenville celebrated its Sesquicentennial in 1947, the Sinclair Building was hailed as "Steubenville's First Skyscraper."

Early Hotels

In big cities, it is often the hotels that vie with the banks to be the tallest buildings. During the high-rise race of the early twentieth century, no hotel tried to outdo the banks in height—though the Imperial and Fort Steuben Hotels did so in elegance.

The Fort Steuben Hotel, in fact, did have a steel-girder skeleton like the big banks, and at nine stories it stood only a floor shorter than the Sinclair. With twice as much frontage, it was actually more spacious than any of Steubenville's banks, but because of its horizontal expanse it did not seem to tower like the "skinny" skyscrapers. Inside, however, it was all luxury. The papers called it "Steubenville's Million Dollar Hotel."

We have already observed that hotels were vital to river towns like Steubenville, and luxury came early. As early as 1798, the tallest building in town was John Ward's United States House on Market Street. Other inns soon followed: Thomas Norton's Black Bear House at Fourth and Market in 1805 and James Collier's Washington Hall on Market Street in 1819. At least half a dozen taverns in business by 1800 were listed as inns, though they only had a few rooms. In his history column in the Steubenville *Evening Star* in 1890, John S. Dike asserted that Steubenville in 1830, with a population of 2,937, boasted eleven hotels. The 1850 Steubenville directory lists thirteen, but the 1875 directory lists only three.

With all the sad stories of Steubenville's great mercantile palaces meeting the wrecking ball, it is gratifying to be able to record a few "happy ending"

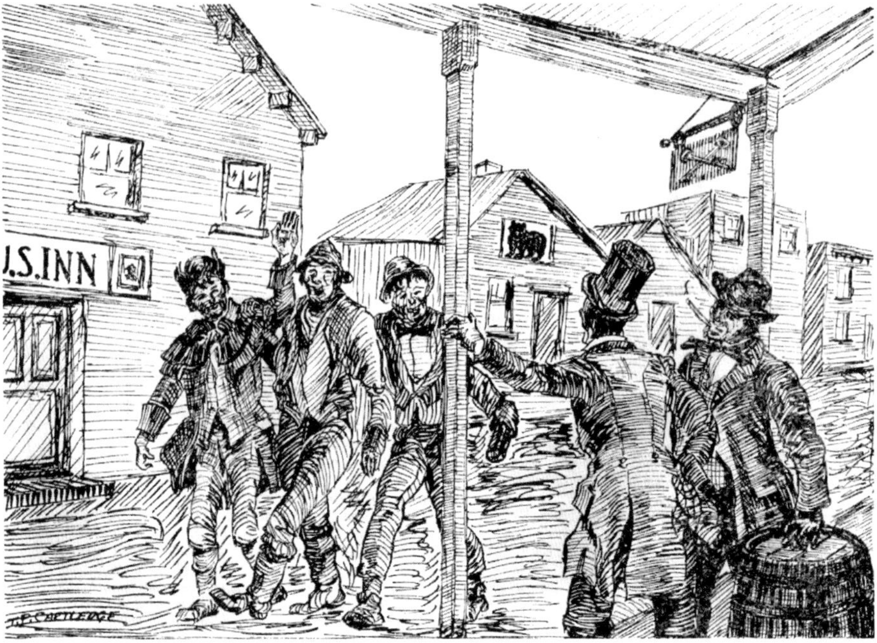

Artist's conception of an early tavern scene in Steubenville, circa 1805. Steubenville Sesquicentennial 1797–1947 Souvenir Book.

stories about Steubenville hotels. The civic pride that made the press and average citizens rally around the bank buildings also made its hotels a source of pride, and its great inns were seen as important links to Steubenville's early days.

In the spring of 1845, however, that linkage was threatened by a young upstart. John Lyle bought John Moreland's defunct tavern on North Fourth, three doors from Market Street, and he tore it down and put up the Franklin Hotel, larger than any of the older inns. Worse, most of the older hotels were in sight of the Franklin and had seen better days. Less than half a century old, the Steubenville hotel industry was already in need of revitalization.

Spurred by the success of the Franklin, the owners of Steubenville's first generation of hotels effected a minor inkeeping renaissance in the summer and fall of 1845. The oldest hotel, the United States (1798), was, aptly, the first to undergo renovation. In May and June, the new owner, James Hanna, added a new three-story wing, nearly doubling the capacity of the inn; he also revitalized the older section. So stunning was the newly reopened United States that the owners of the other older hotels knew that they had to keep up.

They also knew that they would be unable to do so, however. Thomas Norton's Black Bear (1814) desperately needed a face-lift, but Norton was getting old and didn't have the means to give the old inn what it needed, nor was there a new generation of Nortons ready to take over the business. So he sold the business to the firm of Willson and Hooker, which began the second inn restoration project of 1845. Norton was not impressed with the cheap fixes that Willson and Hooker came up with. The patrons of the inn were not impressed either, and they stopped coming to the "new and improved" Black Bear. Thus, only five years later, Norton bought back the inn and leased it to William L. Pennell, who, as the Black Bear's 1850 ad put it, "expended a large sum of money in re-fitting and re-furnishing" it.

The third restoration of 1845 involved the youngest of the first-generation hotels, Washington Hall. This Steubenville landmark was only two dozen years old, but already it was losing its sparkle. What made it worse was that it was the closest of the three inns to the steamboat landing; in fact, it was usually the first building a visitor to the town would see from the wharf. As the face of Steubenville, the Washington had to be revived.

A young businessman named John Hanna bought the old Washington in that fateful summer of 1845—the summer of hotel renewal—and made it once again a Steubenville showplace. The tavern in its basement, the Lamb, became once more the favorite meeting place of Steubenville riverboat captains. Steubenville's oldest hotels were saved for another generation.

They were saved for no more than one, though. By 1875, of the three inns restored thirty years earlier, only one was still in operation: the United States. The only hotels listed in the 1875 directory were the United States, Cochran's on Market between Third and Fourth and the St. Nicholas on the corner of Market and Water—a block closer to the wharf than the old Washington. A few years later, however, Joshua Low would buy two adjoining buildings on Market near Sixth and cobble them together into something that he called the Imperial Hotel.

It did not look very imperial, however. In fact, it scarcely looked like a hotel. So Low kept the three-story corner building, demolished the other and erected in its place a five-story, fifty-room modern hotel annex. Then he built two additional stories atop the corner structure, squared it off with the annex and presented Steubenville with its first five-story, one-hundred-room hotel.

The Imperial, thus improved, stood for another century but not as a functioning hotel. While it remained a Steubenville hot spot well into the twentieth century—its bar, the Revel Room, lived up to its name in the big-band era—the hotel began to deteriorate in the 1960s, and the kind of renovation that saved it in the 1880s was neglected a century later. In

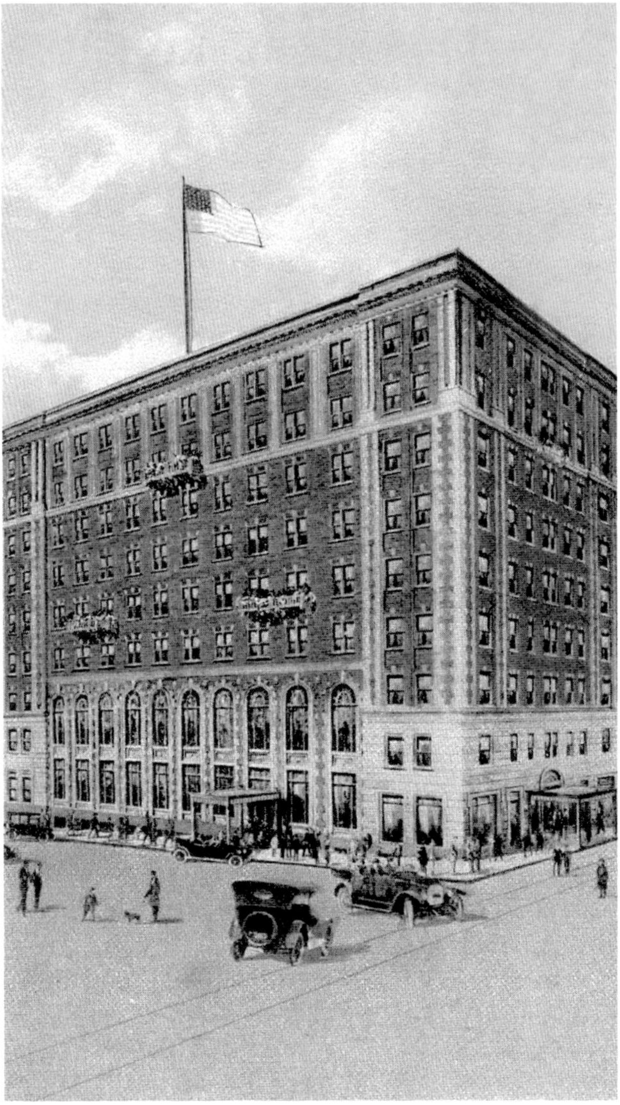

Fort Steuben Hotel, 1921. *Ohio Collection, Schiappa Library.*

January 1998, it was demolished to provide a parking lot for Trumbull Savings Bank.

The same kind of neglect claimed the much newer Fort Steuben Hotel by the late 1970s. Abandoned and closed up like the Imperial, the ceiling of the once-splendid ballroom developed plaster stalactites from condensation and the massive marble pillars were caked with dust. The Fort Steuben found friends that the Imperial had not. A dedicated team of social workers at Marion Manor, Inc., a nonprofit corporation established by the Roman

Catholic Diocese of Steubenville, waded through the full year of paperwork needed to secure a $3.6 million forty-year mortgage from the Department of Housing and Urban Development. They aimed to restore the landmark as a housing center for elderly and handicapped citizens. In September 1986, two months ahead of schedule, the fully restored Fort Steuben Hotel, with its spacious ballroom as dazzling as ever, proved to be at least 3.6 times as good as the "million-dollar hotel" of 1919.

PART VI

Music and Entertainment

Steubenville's First Theatres

Even a decade after the death of the great Hollywood entertainer Dean Martin, the name of that Steubenville native still tends to overshadow all others. Long before Dino, though, there were sons and daughters of Steubenville who made it big on the national stage. Conversely, there were big name stars from elsewhere who played Steubenville's many stages in the heyday of variety and vaudeville.

Though small midwestern cities like Steubenville became punch lines about "playing the sticks" to every song-and-dance team that dreamed of playing the Palace in New York, such cities were also the lifeblood of vaudeville. Every major popular act from the time of the Civil War until after World War II played Steubenville. The peak era of live entertainment in Steubenville was probably 1882–95, when the city boasted three theatres of 800 or more seats (Garrett's Hall and the City Opera House, both over 1,000 seats each, and Weeks' Theatre Comique with 800) and smaller venues such as Philharmonic Hall and Adam Hammerly's London Theatre, each seating about 350. The city itself was briefly in show business at that time, running the City Opera House from 1883 to 1889 and then leasing it to private managers.

As a frontier town, Steubenville might be expected to discover theatre rather late in its history, but precisely because it was a frontier town—to easterners and Europeans on their way to the wilderness, a last glimpse of "civilization"—hotels were thriving in the town's first generation, and innkeepers were anxious to find ways to entertain their guests. In 1819, a Connecticut lawyer and War of 1812 veteran, James Collier, came west to

Steubenville and put up what was then the tallest building in town: a three-story brick hotel known as Washington Hall, which housed a tavern known as the Golden Lamb, a reading room with the latest newspapers and magazines from more than twenty American cities, London and Edinburgh—and Steubenville's first theatre.

A group of Steubenville's literary-minded young men began the Steubenville Thespian Society in Washington Hall in 1820. August Culp was the leader of the group and became its stage manager; Dr. Samuel Ackerly, who ran a private school for boys, directed; and Thomas Cole, apprenticed to his father as a wallpaper designer, painted the sets. They were, doubtless, amateur in quality, but the artists were paid, though, as Cole lamented in an 1823 letter, not enough to cover room and board. Cole would later become the leading landscape painter in America. Alexander Devenney, who would become one of Steubenville's first riverboat captains, was an actor with the group. In 1821, inspired by the Greek revolt against the Ottoman Turks, the thespians began producing the great Greek tragedies (though also many modern plays), with a portion of the proceeds dedicated to the relief of Greek patriots.

As the town grew, other businessmen built high-ceilinged "halls" to compete with the Washington. None of them were yet called "theatres"; these were large multiple-use spaces for dances, political meetings, public lectures or concerts. In 1830, William Kilgore built a hall on Market Street between Fifth and Sixth that would be the premier venue for theatrical events for the next eighty years. In its earliest form it was sixty by forty feet with eleven-and-a-half-foot ceilings; later owners expanded it.

The success of Kilgore's hall spawned imitators. For the next decade, merchants building any kind of business included a public hall to be rented out, usually on the top floor. In 1836, it was D.W. Stier's hardware; in 1839, Kell's Long Room opened with a Christmas ball; and in 1850, William Scott's general store added a hall remembered in the Steubenville Centennial Souvenir (1897) as "for many years…the leading theatre of the city."

In 1851, the year Steubenville was incorporated as a city, two technological developments revolutionized its theatres. The first was the railroad, incorporated that year, though it would be two years before the lines actually entered the city. But the second was in place by the summer of 1851: gaslighting. Kilgore Hall received its gas jets in September, and Kilgore immediately sought to capitalize on the theatrical possibilities of gaslighting by hosting a massive variety show, ostensibly a benefit show for the county's poor but in reality a chance to show off the stage and local talent.

George Kells, partner in Sterling, Kells & Co. Dry Goods and Groceries, directed and starred in the big talent show, which exemplified the type of entertainment that would dominate the American stage under the name of "variety" (1860–80) and later "vaudeville" (1880–1930)—individual, disconnected acts of various types. "Kells' Varieties" opened on Monday, January 11, 1852, and the Steubenville *Mammoth Weekly* reported the performance as "a crowder." The offerings were mostly musical, but Kells himself wrote, directed and starred in a parody of *Richard III* called "Richard Three-Eyes." The crowd (or perhaps the performers) couldn't get enough: they staged a repeat on February 28.

A review of the performance in the *Mammoth Weekly* offers some insight into the nature of the variety stage at the middle of the nineteenth century; Steubenville's experience mirrored the rest of the country. The professional theatre was at pains to distinguish itself from saloon hall entertainment that was decidedly lowbrow, rowdy and usually obscene. Thus an ad for Kells's show announced, "There will be nothing in the entertainment to offend the most fastidious moral taste; consequently, it is expected that a great number of ladies will grace the occasion with their presence." The history of Steubenville theatre in the nineteenth century is typified by a tension between the "fastidious moral taste" and the risqué—with both types of shows appearing on local stages.

The Opera Halls: Garrett's and the City's

Kilgore Hall continued to be the home of the mainstream, more respectable theatre, even after it changed hands in 1869. In 1868, the *Daily Herald* taunted Steubenville because the opera diva Euphrosyne Parepa-Rosa, who was touring the United States with her Grand English Opera Company, played Pittsburgh and Wheeling but snubbed Steubenville for lack of "a hall suitable." She was not being a prima donna, despite the fact that she was, well, a prima donna; Kilgore's stage, the best in the city, simply could not accommodate the huge, multiple sets that a major opera company transported by train.

The following year H.G. Garrett, a prosperous dry goods merchant who was also founder and treasurer of the Union Deposit Bank in Steubenville, was outraged at the insult to his city and decided to do something about it. He bought Kilgore Hall and completely renovated the stage, expanding it to fifty feet wide and thirty-one deep, with ten flats for scenery, trapdoors in the floor and trapeze moorings on the ceiling. Garrett doubled the number of gas jets for lighting to eighty and increased the seating capacity to one thousand. The resulting Garrett's Hall could now stage any production that any eastern road company could throw its way.

For about a decade, Garrett's Hall (later Gray & Garrett's) was the only home in Steubenville of large theatrical and operatic productions from New York and Boston. In 1882, however, Steubenville's city council took a gamble. Convinced that the city could support more than one full-size opera house, the council voted to expand the city market building by adding an upper floor—in the form of a fully equipped opera house. City Solicitor Charles H. Reynolds ran the opera house for its first year. The grand opening was the hit of the New York stage, the melodrama *Lights o'London*, on August 27 and 28. Reynolds struck on an ingenious method of ensuring a large local audience. All of the leads were New York and London professionals, but the director came early to engage and rehearse local actors and singers for the chorus. All of Steubenville turned out to see family, friends and neighbors in a "New York show."

A various and stunning season followed: *Hamlet*, *The Pirates of Penzance*, *Rip Van Winkle*, *Uncle Tom's Cabin*—in fact, several productions of *Uncle Tom* competed at the opera house and Gray & Garrett's (which now called itself Garrett's Opera House to keep up with the city), and other titles that were household names in 1883 but now known only to theatre historians. A production of *Cinderella*, in April 1884, was a technical breakthrough for the opera house, using calcium or "limelight" to spotlight soloists. A technician was brought in from Pittsburgh to run the special light.

STEUBENVILLE'S FIRST CROONER: WILLIAM H. MACDONALD

Although Dean Martin is Steubenville's high-water mark for national celebrity, he was not the first singer from this city to make it big nationally. When Steubenville's opera house premiered, one of the leading American tenors in light opera and operettas (the precursor of the Broadway musical) was William H. MacDonald of the Boston Ideals—born in 1849 in Steubenville, where he received his first musical training (though in his teens he studied for four years in Italy). While MacDonald never achieved anywhere near Dino's level of fame, even by nineteenth-century standards, he did rise to the top in his niche and was, at the end of the 1800s, a household name.

In the late 1870s, when Gilbert and Sullivan's *H.M.S. Pinafore* (1878) and *Pirates of Penzance* (1879) had crossed the Atlantic and had Americanized the British craze, Steubenville's MacDonald, then in his early twenties, was just establishing himself on the Boston and New York stage. In Boston, a woman named Ober brought together the premier church choristers of the city to cash in on the *Pinafore* craze and in 1883 formed the Boston Ideal Pinafore Company. The following year, when they began expanding their repertoire beyond a single Gilbert and Sullivan operetta (though that play alone could have kept them touring for a decade), MacDonald joined them and very quickly established himself as one of the great male leads in that genre.

Unlike so many stars then and now, MacDonald, while staying in the New England and Broadway limelight, did not forget his hometown. Since theatrical companies often shut down in the summer in those pre–air conditioning days, the musicians and directors (in those days nearly exclusively European-trained) were idle three months of the year. Many of the Boston musicians taught at Boston Normal School, but it, too, was idle in the summer. MacDonald saw a way to boost the level of musical education in his hometown. Steubenville's own Female Seminary was also idle in the summer—why not send those German and Italian virtuosi to Ohio for the summer?

So on July 9, 1884, the Boston Normal Musical Institute began operation at the Steubenville Female Seminary. Professor Harry Benson, the rare American in the group, headed the Steubenville Institute since he spoke Ohioan. Steubenville's best young singers (predominantly young women) gave a well-received concert August 11, and in the ensuing years homegrown productions of Gilbert and Sullivan operettas were produced at the city opera house.

Meanwhile, MacDonald continued his career, becoming president of the Boston Ideals. His greatest triumph, however, and the role that would be associated with him for the rest of his career, came after he left the Ideals (always a sad day when someone leaves his ideals) for Broadway in 1891. On September 22 of that year, he opened in the title role of a musical version of *Robin Hood*, which became a sensation and kept MacDonald in Broadway leads for another fifteen years. While he did a variety of roles on Broadway—often romantic foreigners like the Spaniard Carlos Alvarado in *The Serenade* (1897) and the Italian Corleone in *The Viceroy* (1902)—he was identified for a generation with the dashing hero of Sherwood Forest, first in a 1900 *Robin Hood* revival, then in a sequel named *Maid Marian* (1902, though in this he played Little John) and finally his last revival of *Robin Hood* in 1902.

When we tell our children and grandchildren what a great crooner Dean Martin was, we can always back it up with CDs and DVDs and MP3s. Or maybe vinyl or 8-tracks if we can find a museum piece to play them on. But with earlier stars—at least the ones who predated the phonograph—we can only imagine their performances. Fortunately for the curious, however, MacDonald was at his peak in the early days of audio recording. His 1898

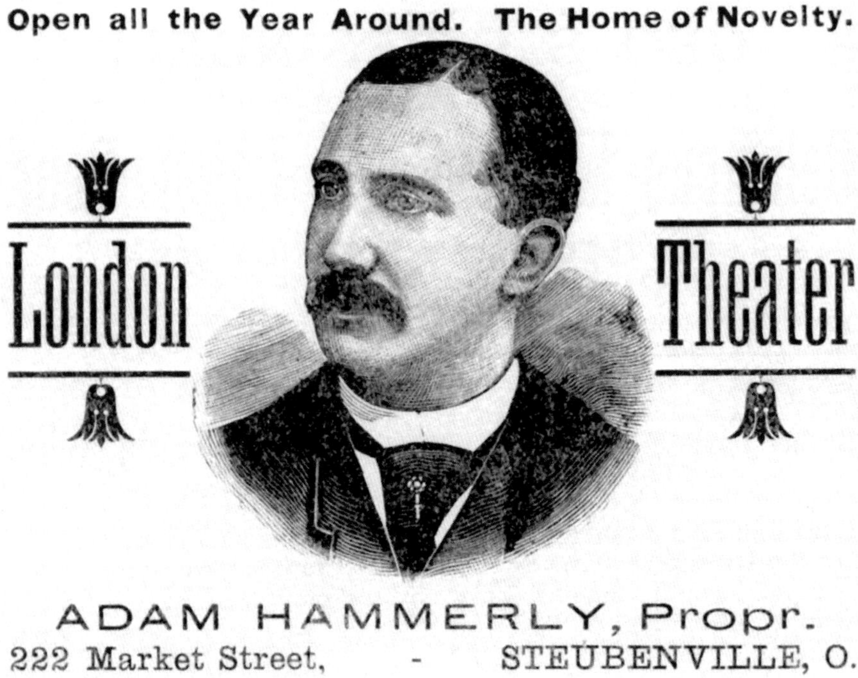

In 1892, when Adam Hammerly ran this (self-) promotion, the London was one of four live theatres with daily shows in Steubenville. *Ohio Collection, Schiappa Library.*

duet "Don Jose of Sevilla" with soprano Jessie Bartlett Davis was recorded by Berliner Gramophone. If you can't find it (or can't afford it) at your antique dealer, you can listen to it for free online.

About the time that MacDonald was breaking in with the Boston Ideals and the city opera house was launched, several less reputable theatres began to flourish in Steubenville. Harry Weeks, who had managed the Tivoli Theatre in Pittsburgh, came to Steubenville in 1883 with his Theatre Comique, which advertised "variety" entertainment but seemed to specialize in female dancers, and in 1890 with Adam Hammerly's London Theater, which offered the same fare. It was then that some Steubenville women decided that they'd had enough.

SOCIAL PURITY LADIES AND THE BURLESQUE

Oddly enough, the offended women did not attack Steubenville's burlesque houses, the London or the Comique. Instead, their target was a one-night engagement at the city opera house of Reeves' English Operatic Burlesque Company, November 21, 1890. The word "burlesque" had only recently begun to take on the "naughty" connotation of women in scanty costumes flouncing like floozies. It is unlikely that Reeves's company intended that type of association, and the Steubenville *Herald* reviews did not make it. But one group of Steubenville women thought it was "that kind of show" and objected.

By 1890, the city's vulnerability to that kind of objection had been considerably lessened. While Steubenville still owned the opera house, it was now leased to professional theatrical managers. After the first successful season as a city venture, E. Roseman Gardner, proprietor of the largest music store in the city, took out a two-year lease of the opera house August 5, 1884, and renewed it for three more years in 1886. On January 12, 1889, more than a year before the burlesque incident, W.D. McLaughlin had taken a five-year lease. It was his problem now.

The leaders of the protest, Mrs. Elizabeth J. Brownlee and Mrs. H.W. Webb, had begun their fight against corruption in the city by opposing demon rum. They had begun the Steubenville branch of the Women's Christian Temperance Union. Elsewhere, when the WCTU had shut down taverns, it had in the process also shut down the crude "saloon girl" shows that went along with them. So an outgrowth of the WCTU was born, the Social Purity Society, and Mrs. Brownlee was the president.

So it was that Mrs. Brownlee and Mrs. Webb went to Mayor Oscar Brashear—who was in the process of watching the show—and demanded that officials arrest the company for offenses to public decency. Mayor Brashear could see that, even if the city's liability were limited, groups like the SPS could cause a public relations disaster for his office if it became too easy to file lawsuits against anything that met their disapproval. At first the mayor was mortified by the women's demands, but then he rallied with a solution. He told the ladies that he could not respond to the complaint without a petition of one hundred witnesses declaring the show immoral and a $500 bond to cover court costs. Luckily, a Steubenville *Herald* reporter was there to record Mrs. Webb's response to the idea of a petition:

> *"Who attend these entertainments?" she exclaimed, "the slums of the city." This aroused the ire of the Mayor, who promptly replied, "Ladies, my wife is in that house, and I want you to understand that she does not come from the slums. There are also many of the very best women in the city."*

Rebuffed, Mrs. Webb and Mrs. Brownlee consulted their lawyers and returned to the theatre close to midnight to say that they would not sue the city but rather would pursue the matter with the manager, McLaughlin. They never did.

The "Flickers"

The end of live shows in Garrett's or the city opera house, however, would not be due to moral censure but to a new medium: the movies. By the turn of the century, both Garrett's and the opera house were showing films, but only as a feature of their stage shows. By 1907, however, the first building in Steubenville constructed exclusively for movies appeared: the Ohio Theatre. The Grand, at 117 South Fourth Street, had been showing films for several years but was a converted vaudeville house, and the lessees, Burt and Nicolai, were dissatisfied with the facilities. So they built the Ohio.

By the end of the decade, there were several movie houses in Steubenville, though most continued to book vaudeville acts as well. In 1909, Steubenville funeral director James A. Lindsay founded the National Amusement Company at 517 Market, where he booked vaudeville acts. In 1913, the National moved to 172 North Fourth, where it built a larger stage, fifty-four feet wide and thirty deep. In 1915, Pittsburgh entrepreneur George Shafer took over the management of the theatre. The same year the Steuben, a new one-thousand-seat movie house, boasted a fourteen- by eighteen-foot screen. Live theatre was becoming rare in Steubenville, as Garrett's became the Rex Theatre and the opera house became the Victoria.

At this time, Hollywood was not yet the major locus of filmmaking. Edison Studios in New York led the pack, and in 1908, Charles Stanton Ogle, son of Steubenville preacher Joseph C. Ogle, appeared in the Edison feature *The Boston Tea Party*. Two years later, he would make movie history by becoming the first actor to portray Frankenstein's monster in the first film version of *Frankenstein*. The film was long lost, but in 1976 it was found in a private collection and partially restored. The coursing electricity of the later movies was not used for Ogle's version—instead, he arose dripping from a vat of chemicals. In all, Ogle would appear in nearly three hundred feature films before his retirement in 1925—four years before sound came in, which is the main reason he is not well known even in his native city.

Most of the films that Ogle was in no longer exist. The nitrocellulose film on which they were made eventually decomposed into nitric acid, which further accelerated the decomposition of the film stock. But one blockbuster in which he appeared was rescued and restored: Cecil B. DeMille's original

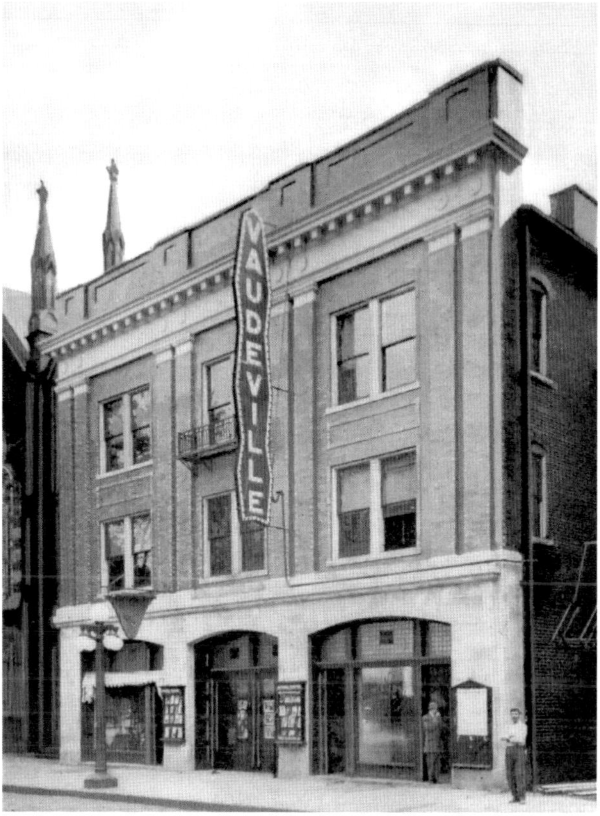

The caption of this World War I–era postcard identifies the *Herald Star* building, but the newspaper is overshadowed by vaudeville—live and film. *Ohio Collection, Schiappa Library.*

1923 version of *The Ten Commandments*, in which Charles Ogle played a doctor in the "modern" scenes.

Steubenville's cinema showcase, however, was the Capitol, which made its big debut on September 7, 1925. Designed to accommodate both live shows and film—the last theatre in Steubenville to do so—this movie palace covered 150 feet of frontage on Fourth Street and 131 feet on Adams. Inside—oh, my! "Palace" was not an exaggeration. A Grecian frieze and Corinthian columns graced the lobby, while over the seats hung a balcony that defied gravity—despite holding twenty-six tons of steel and concrete. Not a single pillar supported the balcony, leaving unobstructed views below; only the engineers knew how it was done.

Conventional wisdom says that movie palaces killed vaudeville and live theatre in general, but just as often they prolonged the life of the live stage, and that was the case with the Capitol. The Steubenville *Daily Herald*'s review of the Capitol's opening hailed the event as the return of live theatre to Steubenville. "Steubenville theater patrons welcomed vaudeville at the

Capitol yesterday, following its absence from local stages for several years," the *Herald* proclaimed. "And they welcomed it vociferously."

All of the theatres at this time sported massive pipe organs. The Capitol's organ would be the envy of the Ohio Valley, but it would not be installed until 1927. Still, the premiere was not silent: a twenty-piece orchestra graced the pit. For the live shows, there were ten dressing rooms and two prop rooms beneath the stage; above the stage was fly space ample enough to drop scenery to the full height of the proscenium. It was so decadent that the Social Purity Society was sure to drop in soon. They did not, but another moral issue was brewing that would, paradoxically, extend rather than end live theatre in Steubenville.

The Blue Laws

By 1930, moviegoing was such a pervasive part of life that its absence on Sundays was beginning to chafe even the most religious keepers of the Sabbath. Sunday afternoons, after church, seemed the perfect time for the family to see a movie. Steubenville, however, still had city ordinances against entertainment establishments—or shops, for that matter—operating on Sundays. In American slang, they were called "blue laws," apparently after the eighteenth-century "bluestockings" who set a high moral tone for culture. The theatre owners asked city council to repeal the law, but council was nervous about possible repercussions.

So, early in June, in an act of brazen civil disobedience, two theatre owners decided to see what would happen if they showed movies on Sunday anyway. What happened was that city prosecutor Jesse K. George had both managers and four employees arrested. It quickly became apparent, though, that popular sentiment was on the side of the movies. The city council moved to strike down the law but had to hold public hearings to ensure that any objections would be heard. In the meantime, Sherriff William Yost posted deputies at all theatres to ensure that the law was enforced as long as it was still on the books. In August 1931, the law was officially repealed, and Sunday movies became legal in Steubenville.

There was a further benefit to come from the repeal of the blue laws, and it was made possible by the magnificence of the Capitol Theatre—though, ironically, during the week of the repeal, another magnificent theatre, the Paramount, opened in Steubenville. It turned out that the city of Pittsburgh held on to its blue laws until well after World War II. Yet the Stanley Theatre in the steel city had contracts with its booking agency that included Sunday performances. So the solution was obvious: continue to book the greatest names in American entertainment, and on Sundays put the whole show on the rails for the easy one-hour jaunt to Steubenville.

The names were big. For about two decades, from 1931 to the early 1950s, the Capitol boasted the top big bands, radio personalities and movie stars. Duke Ellington, the Marx Brothers, Frank Sinatra, Tommy Dorsey, Benny Goodman, the Three Stooges, Orson Welles, Glen Miller, Cab Calloway, the Andrews Sisters, Bill "Bojangles" Robinson, Lucille Ball and Desi Arnaz, Blackstone the Magician, Ella Fitzgerald and Lena Horne—all played Sundays at Steubenville's Capitol.

Hang On, Steubie

When Ohioans swap bragging rights across the river with West Virginia, one of their comparative successes is the fact that pop music fans could never get the West Virginia legislature to declare "Take Me Home, Country Road" (with its opening lyric "Almost Heaven, West Virginia") as its state song, whereas "Hang on, Sloopy" has been Ohio's official rock song since 1985. Many West Virginians will reply that Ohio is welcome to the honor. But actually, there is a Steubenville connection to both songs.

The "Country Road" connection to Steubenville is more tenuous—though so is its connection with West Virginia. The road that inspired the song was located in neither state but rather in Maryland, leading the composers, Bill Danoff and Taffy Nivert, home to a reunion with Nivert's family. Nivert was the Steubenville connection: she was briefly a student at the College of Steubenville, as Franciscan University of Steubenville was then known.

But "Sloopy" has Steubenville roots that touch three generations of musical Sloops in Ohio: two of them in Steubenville. The Sloops were already a musical family before they came to America. Frederick Sloop (or Schlüp) Sr. was born in 1844 in the Swiss canton of Solothurn and apprenticed as a piano tuner before immigrating to America, settling in Findlay, Ohio—right in the middle of the American Civil War. Volunteering at age twenty for the 144th Ohio Infantry, a temporary unit (mustered only one hundred days), Sloop was stationed at Fort McHenry in the summer of 1864 and saw action at the Battle of Monocacy Junction (Maryland) July 9. Mustered out on August 31, Sloop returned to Findlay, where he opened a music store, married a local girl (Victorine Heflick) in 1868 and settled down to raise a big family: Ramona, Leonidas, Leroy, Emma, Marie, Johnnie, Margaret, Ruth, Harriet, Ralph—and Fred Jr.

The younger Fred Sloop might have stayed in Findlay but for the example of another young man from nearby Vanlue—in fact, a regular customer at Sloop's Music—who had made it big in Vaudeville: Tell Taylor. Taylor's song "Down By the Old Mill Stream" would become the biggest hit of 1910. Fred did not have to go to New York, like Tell did, to find vaudeville. Vaudeville was in the process of being eclipsed by movie theatres. For piano players like Fred, this was not a problem. In the first two decades of the twentieth century, most movie houses doubled as vaudeville venues and both needed keyboard players for their giant pipe organs. It was just such a dual-purpose theatre, the Rex in Steubenville, that hired twenty-eight-year-old Fred Sloop Jr. to play for its movies and live shows in 1911.

The income from the theatre was enough to allow Fred Jr. to get married. With his wife, Jane, he moved into a small house at 943 North Seventh and began teaching piano on the side. On September 26, 1913, their first child was born, destined to become the "Sloopy" of Ohio's official rock song: Dorothy Sloop.

As Dot grew up (she would not be known as "Sloopy" for another forty years), her father's musical reputation grew, and she learned at his side. In 1920, Fred and Jane Sloop opened a dance studio, but Fred's piano was in such demand that he found that he had no time to teach dancing, so the studio closed in 1924. As theatre organist, Fred moved up from the Rex to the Olympic Theater in 1918 and then to the Grand in 1926, where he remained until the end of the decade. Then, suddenly, the era of the theatre organist was unexpectedly cut short by the advent of the talkie.

The Sloops should have been devastated. In a city the size of Steubenville —the 1930 census pegged Steubenville at 35,422 people—musicians should have had a hard time finding work once movies went to sound. But by the time they did, Steubenville had a robust musicians' union and plenty of work. Why? Because of what Steubenville old-timers call "Little Chicago."

MIDWEST DIXIELAND

When Prohibition came in 1920, Steubenville's entertainment centers had become, like those in any other American city, magnets for bootleg booze. Anywhere that one illegal activity hides, other illegal moneymakers—like gambling and prostitution—are also found. Also, no one likes to drink or gamble in silence. So by 1929, when theatres no longer needed musicians, downtown Steubenville had a night life worthy of a city many times its size, and that more than made up the difference.

Dot Sloop was a high school junior by then and already almost as much in demand at the keyboard as her father. The range of musical activities at Steubenville High School in 1929 was vast: Dot played piano for the boys' glee club, the girls' glee club, orchestra, chorus and the histrionic club. In addition, she and her sister Margaret—a year younger but in the same class—did a song-and-dance duet for the "S.H.S. Follies of '29" that was such a hit that "the Sloop Sisters" became a highlight of the Follies of '30.

Upon graduation with the class of 1930, Dot took over her father's music school, allowing Fred to devote his hands exclusively to the pianos of the many nightclubs and theatres he played. Despite the downturn already mentioned, movie theatres were not yet totally without musicians, either. Many were still boasting vaudeville acts, and even the houses that could not afford a full orchestra would always want a keyboard player.

Fred Sloop also began sneaking some of his own compositions into his sets with various bands. When his old friend Tell Taylor retired from vaudeville in 1927, Taylor moved back to Findlay and invited Fred to visit him. They started swapping musical ideas, one of which became a catchy song, "Buckwheat Cakes." When Taylor died a decade later, Fred published the song under both of their names, and it became a minor hit in 1939. It was still going strong two decades later as a bit of "old west flavor" on TV westerns, such as "Westward Ho the Wagons" on *The Mickey Mouse Club* TV show. One wonders how many 1950s TV cowboys knew that their campfire song came from two 1930s Ohio guys.

From 1931 to 1939, Dorothy Sloop taught a generation of musicians in Steubenville, many of whom went on to play with her dad at the Capitol or at his regular gigs at the Hay Loft, the Hy-Hat and the Rhythm Club. It was from his band at the Hay Loft that Dorothy Sloop would pick up the Dixieland influence that would make her musical career.

In 1939, Fred had a swinging, hot Dixieland combo with Hamlet DeMatea on drums, Chuck Pierce on trombone, Earl Johns on trumpet and Harry Greenburg on clarinet. Dorothy, who had grown up with jazz, fell in love with her father's pounding improvisations and, pretty adept at them herself, wanted to see if she was good enough to make it in the very home of Dixieland—New Orleans. She was.

In 1939, she joined New Orleans native Yvonne "Dixie" Fasnacht to form a jazz quartet known as the Southland Rhythm Girls, who toured the region. Later in the year, when Dixie and her sister, Irma, opened Dixie's Bar of Music on St. Charles Avenue in New Orleans, Dorothy, now known as "Sloopy" in town, signed on as pianist for the house band.

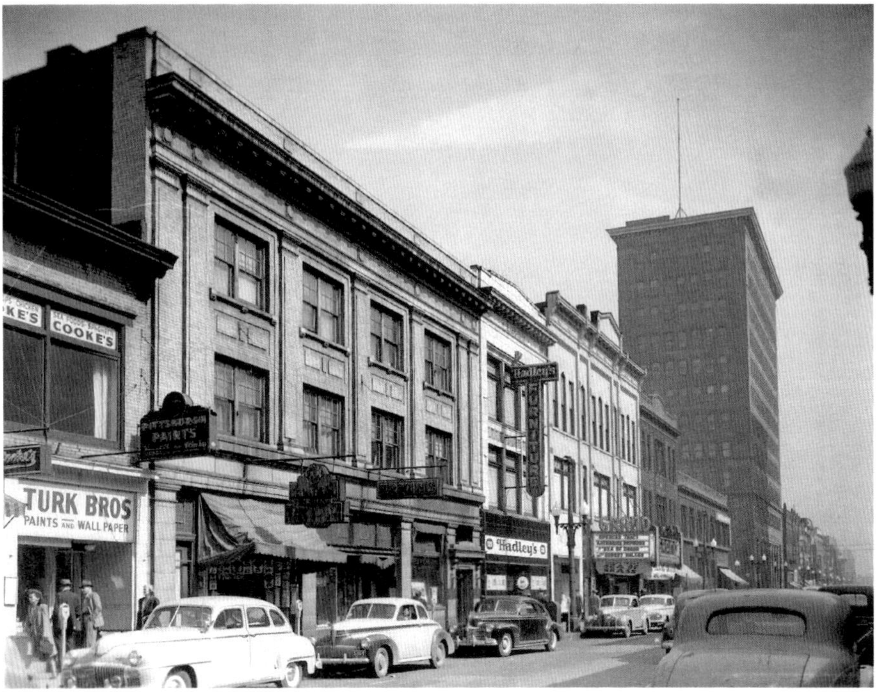

The west side of South Fourth Street, ending at Market. *Ohio Collection, Schiappa Library.*

After hitting it big in the Big Easy, however, Sloopy returned briefly to Ohio right after the war and played in Steubenville's clubs—including the Hy-Hat, where her father had headlined—until 1949. In that year, Dixie moved her Bar of Music to 701 Bourbon Street, and the patrons—a group of jazz lovers that included artists and writers such as Tennessee Williams and Truman Capote—clamored for Sloopy. So once again Sloopy left Steubenville, this time for good, and stayed with Dixie for another two decades, cutting the 1957 album *Dixie and Sloopy* with Fasnacht.

It was during this period that songwriter Wes Ferrell supposedly caught Sloopy's show on a night when she was being inordinately heckled, and supporters yelled out, "Hang on, Sloopy!" Ferrell instantly knew that the phrase was a song in the making, so he wrote it with Bert Russell and sold it first to the Vibrations as "My Girl Sloopy" in 1964, but more famously a year later to the McCoys, who took it to number one in 1965, knocking the Beatles off the charts. That October, a musician in the Ohio State Marching Band, John Tatgenhorst, wrote an arrangement of the hit that became so popular it would be the university's signature tune and, in 1985, the official rock song of the State of Ohio. Sloopy had indeed hung on.

PART VII

Fire and Flood

Hell and High Water

The communal memory of any city is punctuated by its disasters, natural and man-made. For any prominent river city, there are often floods. For the past century or so, federal engineering has offered some safeguards against the periodic rise of the Ohio, but prolonged spring rains or sudden thaws still find residents glancing nervously at the river. Throughout the nineteenth century, Steubenville's newspapers listed the height of the river every day, and everyone in Steubenville turned to that page in the rainy seasons.

In the first part of the century, the town was relatively safe, since the original sixteen blocks laid out by Wells were on high ground. As the town expanded up and down the river, though, its newer, lower streets became vulnerable. In its first half century or so, Steubenville would see the Ohio crest at forty-eight feet three times: November 10, 1810; February 10, 1832; and April 20, 1852. All of those would be forgotten by a flash flood in 1878 that, while not bringing the water nearly as high as those early floods, did more damage.

On September 11, 1878, a rain began to fall on Steubenville that would bring the most destructive flood in the city's eighty-one-year memory. The timing could not have been worse: the Panhandle Division of the Pennsylvania Railroad line had just finished excavation for a large depot to accommodate Steubenville's growing volume of train traffic. By the end of the day on the twelfth, it was a huge lake. P.T. Barnum's circus had been scheduled for a performance on that same day, but the circus train was diverted to the side tracks when the main tracks went under water.

Damage to the railroad was unfortunately not limited to the depot site. Two freight trains bound for Steubenville—Number 18 westbound near Holliday's Cove (present-day Weirton) and Number 19 eastbound at Reed's Mills—provided just enough weight to bring down the washed-out abutments, plunging both engines headlong into rain-swollen creeks.

Both crews were light for such night duty—just an engineer and a fireman each. On Number 18, the fireman was George Priest, a Steubenville tinsmith on his way home after an all-night run—his third in a week. It was about three o'clock in the morning, and Priest was beginning to wonder whether the extra pay was worth it. Especially since the night schedules were statistically more dangerous than the day: Mr. Priest had been in four railroad accidents already, and the insurance agents were beginning to give him the evil eye. Yet they had nothing to complain about, since George had emerged from four successive derailments without a scratch.

As Number 18 approached the Cove Bridge, the West Virginia farmers heard the groan of steel; the crash and splash of rails, stone, locomotive and nine loaded freight cars; and the hiss of steam escaping the ruptured boiler—the creek itself turning to steam as the hot engine slammed into the brown water.

George's lucky streak continued that night. He pulled himself onto the bank wet and bruised but without a scratch. The engineer, John Donavin, had not been so lucky. He had been thrown from the wreck. When George found him, Donavin's head was bleeding and both shoes were split open, with blood showing through the slits. Making his way to the nearest farmhouse, George commandeered a horse and wagon and rushed his engineer to Steubenville for medical attention. He stopped at the United States Hotel because he knew that Doc Stanton boarded there.

George didn't have to wake Dr. William Stanton; in fact, there were two doctors in the lobby, Stanton and Dr. S.C. Shane. The widow Mrs. Moody had come to fetch a doctor for a boarder at her house on Seventh Street, and as she had a vacant room, she suggested that the doctors tend Donavin there. Donavin's scalp required a few stitches, but his feet needed only bandaging, and George Priest was found to have—after his fifth train wreck—not a scratch.

LATER FLOODS: 1884, 1896, 1913 AND "THE BIG ONE," 1936

Only six years later, memories of the deluge of '78 were made obsolete by a new record high-water mark for the upper Ohio—49.1 feet. On February 6, 1884, a combination of rain and a sudden thaw of ice jams sent the Ohio

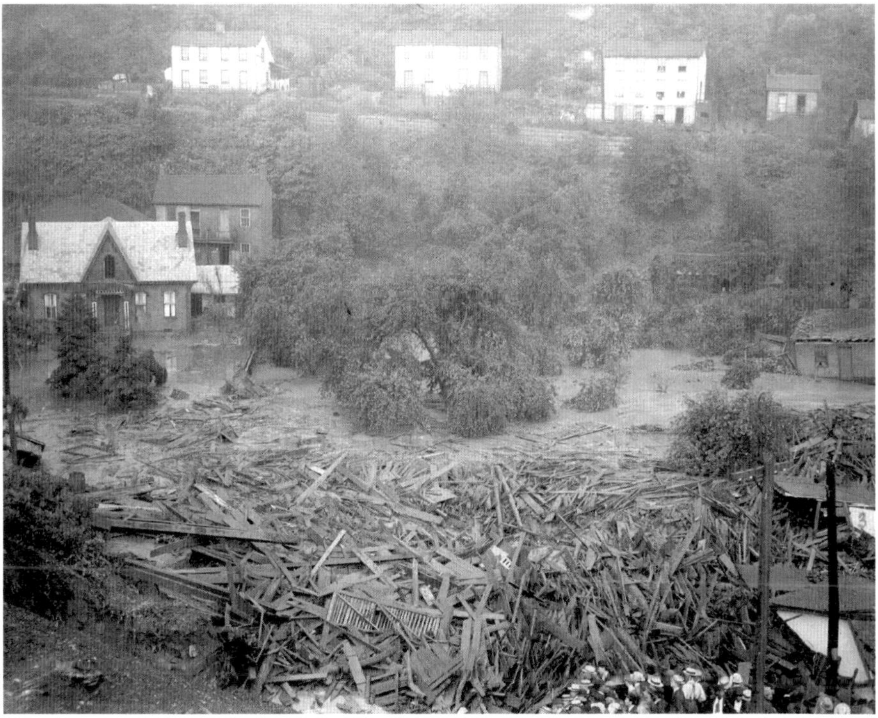

On March 15, 1913, the Ohio River flooded to levels not seen since 1884, destroying this section of Lincoln Avenue in Steubenville. *Ohio Collection, Schiappa Library.*

over its banks. Downtown residents climbed to their roofs and had to be rescued by the *Abner O'Neal* and all other available steamboats.

The next major flood, in the summer of 1896, was not quite as high, but the *Herald Star* called it "the most destructive disaster that has ever visited Steubenville." Shortly after 2:00 p.m. on July 30, 1896, the sky darkened over a Steubenville that had already endured a steady week of rain. The cause of most of the destruction in 1896 seems to have been the erosion of the "Pan Handle Dump." The coal that fueled the mighty steam locomotives produced a great deal of ash, which was dumped over the side of the Pan Handle Bridge at Steubenville, creating a man-made mountain that became the new landscape. This mountain was all but erased by the flood. The overflow from Wells Run and the debris of dozens of houses and barns removed the hills of coal ash. By the end of the day, the pile had sunk by five feet, and railroad officials estimated that three thousand cubic yards of cinder fill were washed away. After the bridge collapse in the 1878 flood, the railroad had constructed a stone culvert to drain floodwaters. The stone itself was ripped out by the debris, which jammed so tightly against the former drain that not even the modern steam equipment could pull it out. Instead, crews blew it away with dynamite and set fire to what remained. The Ohio River below the Jefferson Ironworks was red with the fire for three hours.

On March 15, 1913, the Ohio rose to just six inches short of its 1884 record, hitting 48.6 feet. Wells Run backed up, choking the neighborhoods on Lincoln Avenue with the remains of houses that had been washed out upstream.

The St. Patrick's Day flood of 1936 would break all records, though. Most buildings in downtown Steubenville that had been here in 1884 still bore painted lines marking the water level of that flood. By 11:00 p.m. on March 18, those lines were covered with muddy water, and at 3:00 p.m. the next day, the river would crest at 52.4 feet—a new record. The Ohio National Guard and the Red Cross were dispatched to rescue some seven hundred families, more than 1,500 people, from submerged homes in Jefferson County. The Works Progress Administration (WPA), established by President Franklin D. Roosevelt only the previous year, sent construction crews immediately to clear debris and start rebuilding. The waters began to recede by March 20, but it would be another week before they went below flood stage.

There has been high water in Steubenville several times since then. A New Year's Eve flood in 1942 stopped just short of the 1884 record, 48.5 feet. On March 11, 1964, and September 6, 1990, the scenario of 1913 was repeated as Lincoln Avenue residents were forced from their homes. But the 1936 St. Patrick's Day special is still the champion Steubenville flood—for the time being.

BIRTH OF A FIRE DEPARTMENT

Ironically, it was later that same year, 1936, when the people of Steubenville were trying to forget the dangerous waters, that they tried to remember the dangerous fires. The year marked the fiftieth anniversary of Steubenville's paid fire department, and to commemorate the occasion, the Ohio Fire Chiefs Association held its annual convention in Steubenville in June. For the festivities, Steubenville fire chief Edward J. Green wrote a history of firefighting in Steubenville, which was read at the convention and printed in the *Herald Star*.

What is remarkable about Green's history is not just that it tells the history of Steubenville firefighting from a firefighter's perspective, but rather that it demonstrates the role of specific fires in creating the modern fire department. Historians remember the fires that do the most monetary damage; firemen remember the ones that claim the lives of firemen.

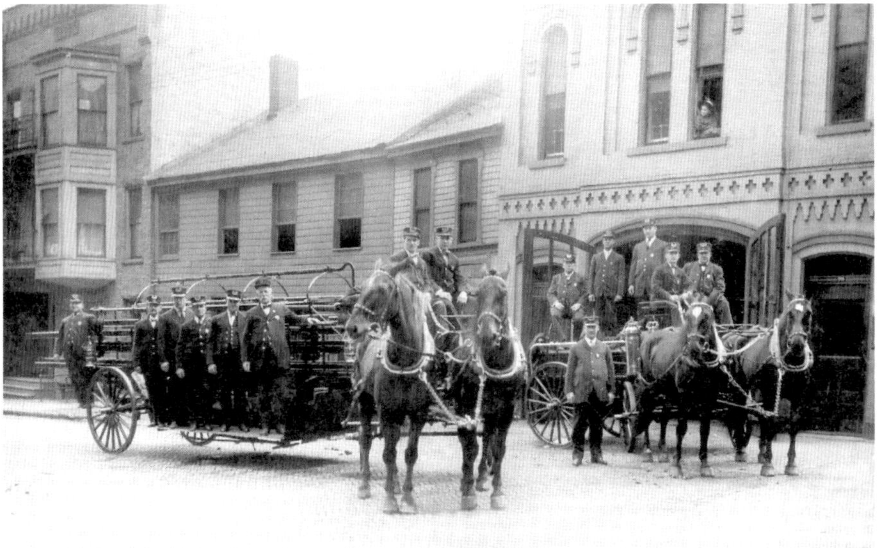

The Steubenville Fire Company, Phoenix Engine House, established 1886. *Ohio Collection, Schiappa Library.*

The United States Hotel fire of March 9, 1885, stuck in the hearts of Steubenville's firefighters for two reasons. First, it led to the creation of the first paid fire department in the city. Second, it led to the death of Steubenville firefighter Alexander Bickerstaff.

Bickerstaff was handling the nozzle of the fire hose that night, trying to keep the flames from the United States Hotel from spreading to the new city building. In the process, the wall of the Cochran Building collapsed, crushing Bickerstaff under a pile of brick and mortar. The tragic death of a brave volunteer spurred Steubenville City Council to create a paid fire department, which officially commenced January 5, 1886.

Epilogue

Dean's Day—and Others

And so I reach the end of my book of stories, realizing all the great stories I have left untold. Yes, reader, I know the one you're thinking of, too. And there's no real reason for leaving it out. Not a single sports hero mentioned, for example, in a city that honors its sports legends. Why is that? No great reason.

If we've left Dino until the end and limited him to an epilogue, it's the same deal: there aren't any Dean Martin Steubenville stories that haven't been told, and told better, by better storytellers. But think about it: if you knew Dino, you know he wouldn't mind. He didn't have that entertainer's need to be the center of attention. He was the king of cool. New York, Vegas and Hollywood were just bigger versions of Steubenville. Nothing he couldn't handle.

So in place of a new Dean Martin story—since I don't have one—how about just a peek at that one moment when Dean came home, the day Steubenville designated Dean Martin Day, October 6, 1950. Just what was it that we were celebrating that day—Dean or ourselves? Were we trying to use Dean as a way of telling ourselves that a guy from Steubenville can go anywhere?

Maybe so, because we know that other show business types started here before and after Dean—W.H. MacDonald, Sloopy, Luigi Faccuilto, Leonard Barr and more.

Luigi who? Leonard who? Well, Luigi was the thirteen-year-old Steubenville kid who replaced Dean in a local gig when Dean had his first big city break in 1938. Luigi went on to sing and dance in over forty films with Gene Kelly and Fred Astaire. It was Gene Kelly who suggested that Luigi teach dance, and so he trained Hollywood's biggest stars for half a century and became the leading name in modern jazz dance.

But while nondancers might say "Luigi who?" many Steubenville old-timers will recognize the name Leonard Barr. No one, perhaps, will remember

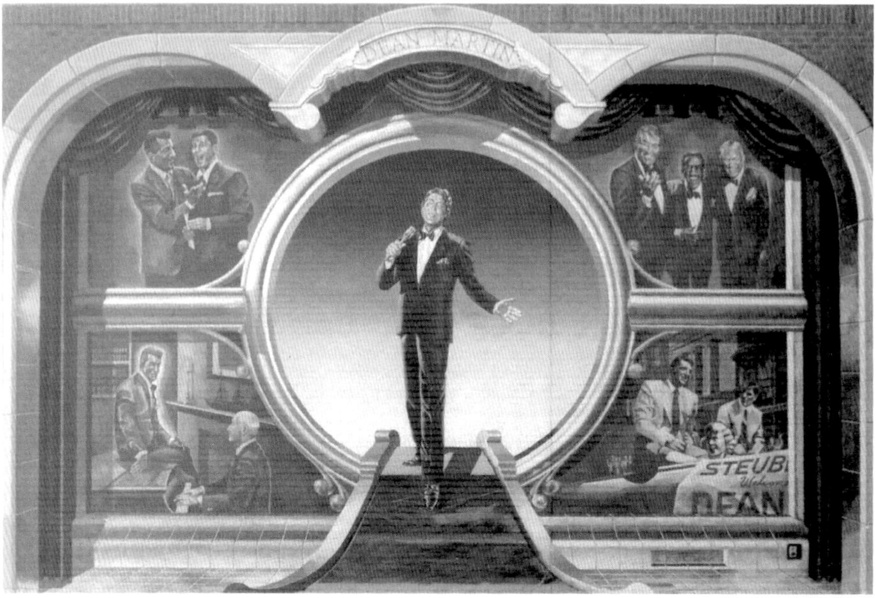

A mural honoring Dean Martin at Kroger City Center, Steubenville. *Steubenville Murals, Inc.*

his vaudeville career in the 1920s, but many recall watching him on Dean's TV show and having the previous generation tell them, "Yeah, that guy's from Steubenville, too. That's Dino's uncle."

Leonard Barr left the Ohio Valley steel mills to hoof it in the waning years of vaudeville as a comic dancer billed as "Bananas." In the 1940s, when his nephew Dean was just coming up, he teamed with Virginia Estes to perform as Barr and Estes, Lunatics of the Dance. It was that act that appeared with Dean in the homecoming show on October 6. But three weeks earlier, on September 17, 1950, Uncle Leonard had appeared as a solo act on the second episode of Dean's show with Jerry Lewis, *The Colgate Comedy Hour*. As long as he was on television, Dean saw to it that Uncle Leonard was working, too.

Is that what Dean Martin Day meant, then? Remembering family? Maybe. But mostly it was Steubenville honoring its own, as it would again in the 1990s, dedicating its most popular mural to the singer and celebrating Dean's birthday every June 7. We love Dean because he was ours, and he made it big. And I don't mind saying "ours," even though I ain't from around here. I don't remember the Steubenville that he called home. Each June, though, when fans from all over the world come to Steubenville to celebrate Dean, I am happy that Dean is the cause for us all to celebrate our past. As the baron would say, *Das ist Amore*. That's *Amore*.

Further Reading

Caldwell, J.A. *History of Belmont and Jefferson Counties, Ohio.* Wheeling, WV: Historical Publishing Co., 1880.

Day, Sandy, and Allen Hall. *Steubenville Bicentennial History*. Steubenville, OH: Steubenville Bicentennial Committee, 1997.

Digital Shoebox Collections: Home. www.digitalshoebox.org. Primary sources for southeast Ohio history, accessed January and February 2009.

Doyle, Joseph B. *Twentieth-Century History of Steubenville and Jefferson County, Ohio*. Chicago: Richmond-Arnold, 1910.

Green, Jerry E. "Steubenville, Ohio and the Nineteenth-Century Boat Trade." *Ohio History* 113 (2004): 18–30.

Holmes, John R. *The Story of Fort Steuben*. Steubenville, OH: Fort Steuben Press, 2000.

About the Author

John R. Holmes grew up in Western New York and studied at St. Bonaventure and Kent State Universities. Since 1985, he has taught English at Franciscan University in Steubenville. His fascination with Steubenville's history began in 1991 when he was asked to portray the city's namesake, Baron Friedrich Wilhelm von Steuben (1730–1794). Dr. Holmes lives in Steubenville with his wife Von and sons Greg, Scott and Luke.

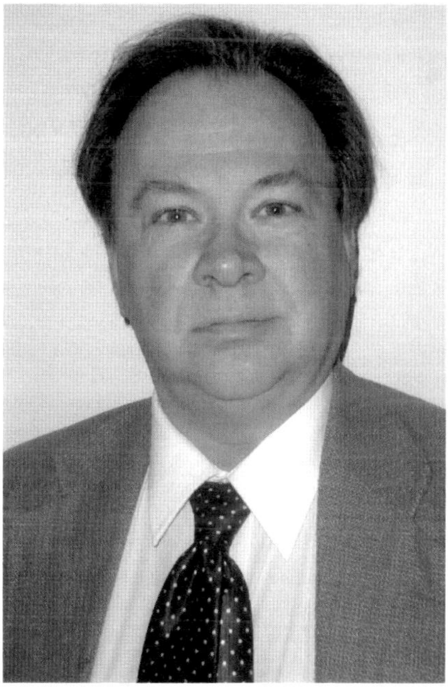